New American Monarch unveils the transformative journey of an individual navigating through the complexities of self-discovery, adversity, and resilience. Through a blend of poignant narratives and vivid poetry, this collection delves into the essence of change, mirroring the metamorphosis of a caterpillar into a butterfly as a metaphor for human growth amidst profound challenges. *New American Monarch* resonates with those at the crossroads of identity, offering a reflective and empowering exploration of the struggles and triumphs that define the path to personal evolution. This book is a testament to the beauty of becoming, which we always are, inviting readers to embrace their own journeys of renewal and the profound realizations that accompany the process of transformation. —**JAVON JOHNSON**, AUTHOR OF *KILLING POETRY: BLACKNESS AND THE MAKING OF SLAM AND SPOKEN WORD COMMUNITIES* AND *AINT NEVER NOT BEEN BLACK*

Nature is available to us, is family to us, so that we might know ourselves better. Marcel Fable Price knows that to confront is to erupt and to name is to detonate. He brings the chrysalis and the communion wine, a birthing story and a lamentation. With *New American Monarch*, Fable Price understands and accepts, perhaps even at great risk to himself, that the only way out is through, and that ruptures are foundational to metamorphosis. This book is an invitation to revel.
—**DOMINIQUE CHRISTINA**, AUTHOR / EDUCATOR / CONCEPTUAL INSTALLATION ARTIST

Marcel uses extended metaphor, both within each piece and across multiple poems, with the grace of a robin landing on a street sign. He explores a multitude of themes in this work, such as grief, gentrification, becoming unapologetic, and detoxifying one's behavior, but he unites them as he explores the topic of change. If the change isn't for the better, it teaches us a lesson, or makes us stronger.
—**ANTHONY MCPHERSON**, POET / DANCER / MUSICIAN / WRITER

Marcel Fable Price returns with a fresh and inspired collection of poems. In this anthology, Fable delves into his personal evolution, truly living up to his name. This collection is a beacon of innovation, offering readers hope and insightful reflections. It explores the intricacies of confronting the past, embracing the present, and striving for personal growth and evolution. —**MASAKI TAKAHASHI MASAKI**, 2022-2024 LANSING POET LAUREATE, FOUNDER OF THE POETRY ROOM

It is always fascinating to watch great talent humbly displayed on a variety of platforms and environs by an individual. Marcel Fable Price has negotiated not only multiple arenas of the scribe and wordsmith, but the mind and soul; balancing the struggles of grief with joys of achievement while still finding growth. Marcel's work as a writer-performer and community organizer has more than earned him the titles of champion or laureate, also friend and comrade.
—**BILLY TUGGLE**, TEACHING ARTIST / PERFORMANCE POET & SLAM CHAMPION

NEW AMERICAN MONARCH

NEW AMERICAN MONARCH

❋

AN INTROVERTED CATERPILLAR'S GUIDE
TO BECOMING AN INTROVERTED BUTTERFLY

❋

MARCEL FABLE PRICE

NEW MICHIGAN PRESS
TUCSON, ARIZONA

NEW MICHIGAN PRESS
DEPT OF ENGLISH, P. O. BOX 210067
UNIVERSITY OF ARIZONA
TUCSON, AZ 85721-0067

<http://newmichiganpress.com>

Orders and queries to <nmp@thediagram.com>.

Copyright © 2024 by Marcel Fable Price. All rights reserved.

ISBN 978-1-934832-96-7.

Design by Ander Monson.

Cover art by Esan Sommersell. Section image title page art by Piper Adonya. Other interior images by Steve Weatherbie.

MARCELFABLEPRICE.COM

CONTENTS

Foreword   xi

Dedication   1
Intro to Metamorphosis   2

Section 1: Pupa   5

The World Through Yellow Aviators   6
Press Pause   8
Collateral Damage   11
The Secret to Rock Paper Scissors   12
Crime Mob 46:16   17
Vision So Bad That...   20
Kanye 3:20   24
Man vs. the Machine   27

Section 2: Chrysalis   32

Kehinde   33
Parallel Systems   37
Rubik's Cube Shinin'   39
Waiting to Be Judged   40
Updated Definition 1   42
When the Gun Wears Blood; Where Do I Place My Fear   43

That Mourning   45
Updated Definition 11   49
When I Die   50
Back in the Day   54
The Frayed Edges of My Black Card   58
Lost and Found God   59
Self Portrait of the Caterpillar as His Grandfather   61
Metabolization   63

Section 3: Transformation   65

More Flavor Than a Good 'Yo Momma' Joke   66
Playing, Just for You   69
Love Is   75
What a Wonderful World   79
The Stories They Share   82
Rosewood Sonnet   87
Terrifying Truths   88
The United States vs the Court of Public Opinion (TCOPO)   90
Fall on Gold   94
Race Together   98
Tour Log   103
Butterfly   108

Acknowledgments and Notes   113

FOREWORD

Representation matters. Reflection is important. Growth is imperative. Grief reaches us all. Survival, by any means necessary is essential, even if it eventually means separating yourself from others, cocooning yourself from the outside loud world, and accepting the adjournment and gavel from The Court of Public Opinion. We've always been told, it doesn't matter if you win or lose, but how you play this game called life.

Dear Little Brother, and reader, this book is poignant. It's a level up that only comes from experience and learning that experiences are always our greatest teacher. The New American Monarch, from the Mind of Fable, is an emotional I.V. drip for those dehydrated by society's views of us and rules for us. This work of art dives into how we respond to shit, the acceptance, denial, the internal conflict and confrontation of things out of our control. But it's also dissecting how we're feeling at the time of individual events that become core memories until they are rungs on the ladder of self discovery and what it means to lose what you love the most.

Marcel Fable Price is one of my best friends, he is the godfather to Josie Symone Foster my daughter. He is the loving widower of Nika Marie Price, he is an avid learner, teacher, community organizer, and co-founder of The Diatribe. He is an incredible poet, writer, and the most reliable person I have ever met in my life and I love him. He continues to overcome every obstacle that tries to negatively define who he was versus who is becoming. Since we started our journey of friendship, business endeavors, and artistry we have both led, followed, fallen, and trusted each other even when we could not see eye to eye, we've always been able to support each other regardless. This book is his emergence from one of the roughest, toughest periods of his life thus far; A pandemic, the loss of a cousin, the loss of a friend and old roommate to cancer, to quitting cigarettes and alcohol, through two bouts of cancer that his wife and our loving friend did not survive, the loss of a show, the adverse effects of medication, the loss and grief of a grassroots organization, a community that could not see nor understand his battles, saying goodbye to those once called friends and family, selling the house that love built and died in, to his private life being put on blast by people and their opinions, and now leaving to start over somewhere new, this book is about breaking out of the cocoon and becoming whatever you decide!

Three things I always say are:

"I'm not for everybody!" You are not!

"You can say or do anything you want but you gotta be ready for the consequences and repercussions!" You know this!

"The right book might save your life, what if it's the one you wrote?" You're still here!

To conclude this foreword I say, Fuck Reverse, well done Little Brother, I love you, and your wife is proud of who you are becoming, you beautiful fucking butterfly!

Enjoy, reader.

Peace Fam!

—Foster

(Gregory Foster II A.k.a. Auto)

DEDICATION

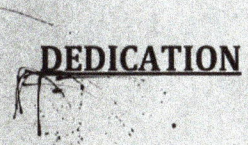

This collection is for the people who can find God within the non-secular stained glass of a butterfly's wingspan.

Who see the imagination of people like Hebru Brantley, Kehinde Wiley, and Ebony Patterson as the windows of our church.

Who look to our communities to be walls that defend our freedom to worship; finding makeshift pulpits on street corners and stages.

Who hear the gospel in hip-hop, and understand pastors ain't nothing more than rappers with a different cadence.

Who understand the dialogue is rooted in the same stories, Moses just has a different sea.

Who understand we are all caterpillars until we aren't. This is for you, larvae. Looking for meaning in the crawl, waiting to find the words that help you comfortably devour yourself.

I hope that one day
you'll be ready
to fly.

[INTRO TO METAMORPHOSIS]

Once it hatches, a caterpillar
will first start to feed on the egg
in which it was born; then, the leaves around it.
In twelve to twenty-four hours it will shed its skin.

                                           It will repeat this process multiple times
                                                                      so that it can grow.

But once big enough,
hormones will dictate when it is "full".
It will stop eating just before it is ready to
make the final transformation.

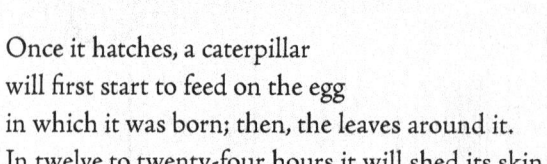

                             It will choose a spot under a covered location
                                                   and build a chrysalis.

This feature stage
is called Pupa.
Before Open Mics
appear on the canvas,
you can witness
larvae break itself into nothing
in empty hungry rooms
that crave slumber from depressives.

                                                     The way bile craves change
                                                   before it takes flight or fight.

Under stage lights,
you can sit front row and bask in awe
as it devours itself.
After fifteen days,
or as long as it takes
to find wings within the chaos—

a butterfly emerges.

This series of changes in this creature's lifespan is called *metamorphosis*.

1 / PUPA

From the book of Fiasco

FIASCO 40:31

Those who have faith in Themselves
    become empowered by their gift.
They will kick-push, until they can carry two;
    they will be hell-bent on healing.
Lord willing;
    they will end up feeling whole.

Thoughts: What if the book began in the era we grew from? What if you felt that inspiration through the chapters? Is that possible? If so, how can we blend it all together sonically?

[THE WORLD THROUGH YELLOW AVIATORS]

Let's not focus on the ugly
this time, eh? Here, the world looks
different. Everything glows
with wonder, still appears to be
middle school innocence.

Not so much
mimicking-spin-the-bottle-while avoiding-eye-contact
but clean-game-of-tag-before-the-cootie-shot.

'Least that's
how it *should* look.

Let's imagine that cross-shaped cloud
outside of your window is really a biplane.

Let's—just this once—not seek out metaphors
of crucifixion, or find parallels
in storylines that remind us Jesus
was just another Black boy
with Tuskegee frames, eyes chock-full of imagination.

Remember when racism
was still an unfamiliar shape?
Intentions still a white linen
on melanin skin, unaware of how
a cotton pillowcase becomes a ski mask?

For once, after way too long,
let's spread our arms and not be staked
to our decisions, but run clumsy-dumb,
stupid-fast, making airplane noises: the only iron in our bodies
jet fuel coursing through our veiny arms

far too busy mimicking wings to ever worry
how metal pierces palms.

Let's turn our sound effects into psalms.

19:1—a *Woosh* or *Vroooom*
as we watch Hebru
create denomination-less hymns with those hands

that let us take a chance
on childhood fearlessness; before cigarettes
on cigarettes, before burn holes
cured by cocoa butter kisses.

   Let's go to church
in the memories of when it was just that
simple, and the sky seemed endless.

   This is where I see God.

Psalm 19:1

The Heavens declare the glory of God;
The skies proclaim the work of his hands.

Hebru Brantley depicts brown children in all their glory; through multiple mediums he tells ballads of their bravery.

[PRESS PAUSE]
A.K.A. "PUSHES ME".
B.K.A. "HEY WHITE BOY"

I was 5 foot nothing—
60 lbs at most—
hype off of Captain Crunch in the lunch line & for the fifth time this month

this guy decided to push me.

He said: "Hey white boy!"   Pushed me.
"Your dad doesn't line you up?"   Pushed me.
"You're wearing the same clothes
as yesterday!"   Pushed me—

proceeding to press buttons causing flashbacks
as if my temper had a DVR—no VCR, we were far
from taping episodes of *Good Times*,
                                    cause, well—
the bad times always seemed more worth remembering.

Plus, the only "Willis" I was watching was Bruce because being
A tough guy, is way cooler than carrying dirty laundry
and I don't know about you, but since then I have always hated
airing out my dirty laundry.

Next day he said
"Hey white boy!"   Pushed me.
"Your dad doesn't line you up?" Pushed me.
"You are wearing the same clothes
as yesterday!"   Pushed me—

but I pressed pause. Because
another day of fast forwarding through hallways takes tolls on the soul. If I
had change to pay tolls, then I would take an easy pass—or a bus to the past.

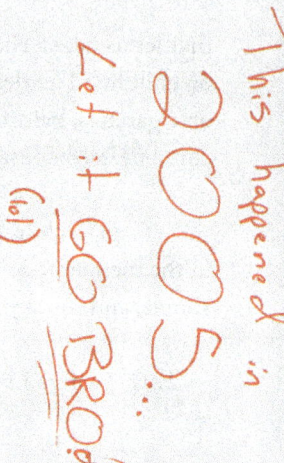

This happened in 2005... Let it GG Bro! (lol)

my right outweighing my re's—son
(reason) Myre-ason to re- route?

Well I was changeless with no clothes, I was broke
& it would show as the holes
in jeans started to outweigh the holes
in my pride & I
was left just hoping I could find another pair of clothes.

But then again— for now the seventh time—
he said: "Hey white boy!" Pushed me.
"Your dad doesn't line you up?" Pushed me.

"You are wearing the same clothes as yesterday!"
Pushed me. I opposed

the *pause* button this time; I grabbed a lunch tray and yelled
"Bitch!" **WACK!**
Followed by a "Wu-Tang Clan Ain't Nothin' to fuck with!" **WACK!**
"I HAVE A SINGLE" **WACK!**
"MOTHER" **WACK!**
"WE HAVE TO SHOP AT GOODWILL, MOTHERFUCKER!"

People really said this sxxt...

We had no clue what the internet was going to be, clearly.

Also, we really were kinda fxxked up...

But it was irony at its finest
when you think about it, because now we have
the white boy in *Good Will Hunting*.

I remember teachers saying something about
sticks
and stones will break your bones, but words will never harm you—

Skip that— do you think razor blades kiss
skin because words are NERF guns? I have played
with NERF guns, & if bullies chose styrofoam
instead of shooting down others' weaknesses
with cheap shit

it seems more likely that events like Columbine
would leave less kids secretly thanking the little man
for finally standing up.

I wish I had told my third grade English teacher

                                               Thank you

for teaching me cursive and frowning on all my cursing
but nowadays I use profanity way more than curly
letters, & I can solve a naysayer's problem with me

with a *fuck you*   so fuck you
if you think that chip on your shoulder is served best by dipping
into other people's insecurities.

We are raised & taught to dodge stone throws, & *just let those haters talk, they will
make you famous*

I just *wish* I could walk around with a Nerf gun.
Scratch that—   I wish I could walk around
with a crossbow and see who opposed my mindset.

I wish schools taught confidence.
Scratch that—   I wish gym class taught
Jiu Jitsu to lift those who didn't feel they were strong enough to defend
themselves.

But most of all
I wish I didn't remember him saying: "Hey white boy!"
as he would push me.

Yet, I am glad
    that I hit
        record.

[COLLATERAL DAMAGE]

Too many of us were infants born
    of hurricanes. Failed to realize
        destruction; our wind
            blowing recklessly
                onto passersby. Failed
            to grasp that being raised
    by natural disasters
        doesn't give us
            the right to be
                someone
                    else's
                      torn-
                          ado.

[THE SECRET TO ROCK PAPER SCISSORS]

Where I am from we learned to play the game young:

rock

        paper

                scissors

                        shoot

Before we ever knew
that taking an extra second
would also mimic the dynamite
that could very well cheat the equation

we were stationed in the school library on career day,
fighting for places in line as if our place in life
would be decided that very day.

    Not so far away
you would hear: "Ceon cut me!"

Little did we know, it was irony. Each step
foreshadowing ones most would never end up taking,
and more than MANY would even attempt to—

                        shoot

unless it was in the direction of the principal's office, because being suspended
is a feeling you get used to when you are constantly hanging yourself by your
actions:

    Detention slips become coat
    hangers to Carhartt jackets
    foreshadowing the work you would
    proudly put into them
    bearing your heart on your sleeve

with ease, sewed in with a tightrope
wire-turned-noose

Why didn't anyone teach us to call for scissors then?

When they could have been used to free our mind
instead of trapping our still-youthful spirit; flaunting those blades
best kept open
like wings spread, ready to fly...
yet to not call for scissors

with pride, in fear of closing them.
Closed, and index falls gracefully upon the middle finger
It will look like the route many took
their whole life anyway...

I am terrified of calling scissors

I can still hear it: Michelle screaming, "Ceon cut me!" And him replying, "Snitch,
how 'bout we play for it!"
But she already knew:
rock
    paper
        scissors
    rock
        paper
            scissors
    rock
        paper
            scissors

Rock. She wanted to be a doctor. Understood
nothing is more valuable than rock-solid plans
by an obsidian woman. To this day, she has
a brother staring at a headstone reflection

who unfortunately called scissors
his whole life.

They used to teach us to be an element in the equation instead of preparing ourselves to be the razor sharp statistic paralleling us in the mirror

That if enough of us focus on a strong foundation,
then we would be the granite that stabilized our generation enough to come to a future we never intended on living long enough to see.

But, far too many of us would succumb to our surroundings, leaving us pre-packaged products of our environment

Where I am from, mass production could have been the prom theme.

Little girls were balloons, blowing up with life,
except the hot air only slipped from lips of boys
who would never tend to their responsibilities.

Leaving scissors the only viable option after school dances.

You can only look at the balloons for so long,
Before you notice that you still aren't   shooting
for the stars.

You see,
they never teach you to call paper—
hiding the fact that you can be a rapper,
novelist, photographer, rock star, painter, poet—
behind textbooks and social standards
as showing the youth

"You can be anything you put your mind to"
Instead of the school to prison pipeline—
Seems almost scarier to our public school administrators
than the lyrics, in the music, on the paper
some of our youth are hungry to become.

Somehow, I called paper.
I always call paper. I had to,
hearing art and creative writing not being referred to as "real classes" all while
mandatory to the curriculum
doesn't sit well on a mind stretched this paper
thin. This fragile, this skin
isn't ready for a bullet.
I could never call

                scissors

                            shoot

because   scissors

                        shoot,

get shot, or get locked up.
My best friends Keenan, Ceon, Harry;
or Kyron who piled scissors on an elderly woman for her purse.

To this day, I want to ask him: "What was it worth"?

If it ended up heavier than the burden on his soul,
And if so...
If he knew the American Dollar is really worth nothing...
As I am sure he is worth more than that.

We were all taught this equation all to well.

They say

        scissors
beat   paper

Look at the *drug dealers* feeding the creative
popularity of gangsta vs. conscious rappers
or the stigma of bullies vs. the band kids.

They say

        paper
beats rock

Putting in those years you could have committed
to an unpaid internship, in turn
allowing your artistic talents to soar,
not forcing yourself to fight through cogs
in a system not built tough enough
to chewing through the false narrative
that you can't survive on your passion—Croche

Paper proving everyone wrong who said that it was smarter
to pursue years of school while collecting debt.
Instead of learning to monetize your gift,
know that you are one.

"Rock beats Scissors"
Being a lawyer is better than being a "criminal",
Being a cop wins vs. a "thief",

But what about those educators stealing dreams
Lookin' scissors,
Dressed as textbook rock.

So the cycle never stops,

And until it does, it is on us.

So Rock, Paper, or Scissors—

What will you show your peers it is safe to become?

[CRIME MOB 46:16]

"Knuck if you buck boy..."

But low key, Varian said I was that I remember getting washed.

The co-teacher of this Middle School Masculinity program said something to our class that I, at the time, couldn't fully grasp. He explained that masculinity means understanding that your wide array of emotions and actions are as necessary as a tool belt. *Many of you only use hammers; how stable would a home be if you only use a mallet to construct it?*

The first time I did it, I used words. I hadn't yet visited my innocent adolescence bestowing me with that unforgiving fire that erupts in your belly when your ears are assaulted by a certain verbiage. I was seventeen; he was hooking up with my best friend's sister and tried spittin' game at a woman I was seeing.

I called him up. When he answered, every bigoted phrase for a Latinx person that I could think of rolled off my tongue like a confederate flag unfurling in a rural backyard. His response was something that would stick to me like a birthmark, or a horrible tattoo you can't afford to live down much less take off:

Bro. Bro, me and my cousins are going to beat your fucking ass, Bro.

They did. [They straight whooped my ass, nailing me to my cheap verbal attacks, luckily leaving the other tools at home] And I deserved it. But still, I didn't fully learn.

I have always been a metal spike, even before I tasted pennies in my mouth. Since age five when a hammer came down on my life and put me to use until I was seventeen. But he didn't do it out of anger; retaliation wasn't the momentum behind his downfalls. I understand his father handed down this treatment in the same toolbelt his father's father once gifted him, but as a contractor he should understand that erecting a stable environment isn't done through demolition.

Maybe he assumed my foundation was corroded, because—don't get me wrong—he wasn't a bad stepfather unless he was three sheets deep or five fingers balled and swinging, teaching me "life lessons" by pounding me deeper into my surroundings.

Or maybe, it was because I had too much blackness, too much creativity, not enough him. So he imbedded what he could of his own in me: his upbringing.

I needed therapy FRFR

The next time I did it, the words were coming at me. The next time, I was the answering fist. I was the alchemy of nail-become-hammer. I was about to be afire with that rage that burns hot and long in your stomach when you hear something uttered that utterly sets you off.

I was twenty-two, at a house party in the white-washed boonies of West Michigan, in the act of lighting one of my Newports on somebody's back porch. That night, I was drinking to excess in a neighborhood where the name General Lee barrels off pale tongues that have never felt comfortable around me. No predominantly white neighborhood had ever opened itself comfortably to me. [So I drank and smoked and hoped I didn't get nailed by the predominantly white cops that always accompanied them.]

I was taking my first drag when this Malibu's-Most-Wanted, wannabe Real Slim Shady kid walked up. He obviously thought he was NWA but resonated with me like Little T and one track Mike. He had a 40 oz. in hand, t-shirt down to his knees, and team Jordans on—which, in my eyes, was already an abomination—and said:

Yo. Yo, you got another Nigger Mint?

All I could do was stare. And then turn my back and walk away. I wandered inside, dazed. I thought: he couldn't possibly have intended... I thought: surely he just... But with every step, my hunger grew. Every stride battered that hard "r" deeper into my mind. I thought: there's no way this kid has never noticed that the rap songs he emulates throw on an "-a."

But here I was in the middle of Bush country, not to mention Busch country: the only splash of color this house had ever seen besides its beige walls. My face felt hot and my eyes had begun that nervous frustrated twitch they do when I feel like I'm about to have a panic attack. One of the three friends I had come with saw me standing there, struck speechless, and asked what was wrong. When I told him that I was pretty sure some thin-lipped ivory-colored kid had decided to label my square a 'Nigger Mint,' he blessed me with:

Well, shit. If you gotta beat his ass do it. But lemme let the homeowner know. And first, make sure he said it.

So I did. I made sure he'd said it. With a fire in my body and my fingers twitching for something like a hammer, I walked back outside, pulled out my smokes, and said—in my best interview-with-a-white-manager voice:

My bad my friend, I must be buzzed up. Did you request something from me? I could have sworn you needed something.

I was really channeling my inner Andy Griffith. It was all I could do to keep a stranglehold on the bellows stoking my rage. And this Dustin-Diamond, this Mark-Zuckerburg-with-a-fitted cap had the audacity to once again utter:

Yeah... a Nigger Mint.

There it was again, complete with that fully-pronounced "-er"—like he couldn't help but extract his forefathers' genes, even while wearing Girbaud denim. I lost it. I raised my hammer high and brought it down on the skinny nail of his face.

While using a screwdriver earlier this year, I truly paid attention to it for the first time. I watched the metal ridges displace splinters as they curled out of their once-home. I'm learning I can use my sharpness for stability. I can ease it gently into the right places and the joints will hold. I'm thinking I'll keep adding to my toolbelt; maybe a saw, for carving away the rotten pieces I no longer need. Someday, maybe I'll even snag a tape measure to hold up against myself, to show my stepfather how I've grown.

[VISION SO BAD THAT...]

At ten years old,
          I tried to hit a
          soda can that was five
          feet away, with a
          B.   B.   gun—
          started to realize that
          I could not read the words
          "Coca—Cola" on it, pulled
          the   trigger anyway,
          failing to   make
       the connection.

[handwritten: Seriously though, I am legally blind...]

Realizing

    A. I might need glasses, and
    B. If you can't see, you
       probably shouldn't be trying
       to shoot things.

But what I did peg was a two-inch-wide oak
by mistake.

Following this experience
was my first visit to the optometrist.
Glasses have not always been
as "in" as they are now.

I, wielding a rat tail and high top fade,
was dreading this experience.

The frames bestowed upon me were
a decadent blend of what can only be described as
an infusion of leopard print & tortoise shell—

an amalgamation of two creatures that nature
would *never* allow to make love.

Why? Because that would make one hideous creature,
one that just happened to make a home on my face.

I arrived at school the next day,
a new boy.

Students trumpeted upon my entrance:
    "Family Matters in the building!"
    "Steeeeeve!"
Laughter, a marching band
that paraded behind me through the hallways.

The ballad I heard most often:
    "Did I do thaaaaaat?!"

Over time, I learned to become one with the noise;
grab a sax and Coltrane my nature into *boys will be boys*—

Every year my vision got worse, my lenses protruded more.

Freshman geography class:
    "Your glasses are so thick, when you look at a map, you know the weather."

Over here like:
    "It's about 72 degrees in Denver" -lookin' boy.

    At seventeen,
I couldn't see the pellet
in the bark   anymore.
That year in biology
I l e a r n e d that

                    a tree will continue to grow—
                    even with something foreign
                    embedded in it. Glasses
                    e x p a n d i n g each year,
                    mimicking the ripples flaunting
                    a tree's telling of a g e.

I want to ask the oak if toxic
masculinity is a little like that extrinsic object
it now nurtures as its own; how it ended up growing
to protect something that at one time damaged it most.

I still don't know if I'm the projectile
or the tree in this metaphor.

But I know that I've had a mouthful of copper
and seeds since I learned how to bury them both.
Clench my fists along with my teeth,
and break them on the too tough to swallow.

I mastered the art of deflecting everything.
I wasn't a womanizer; I just wasn't ready to slow down.
I am not a player; I just wasn't built to be monogamous—what they don't know
     won't hurt.

Pops ghosted; and I was alright.

I don't like fighting, I just enjoy shutting people up. (Especially Nazis)

Yo, my glasses are so thick, I can look forward and see the Lions win a super
bowl.

Turn them around, see Barack's inauguration.
Flip 'em back, see Michelle's.

Funny how I got all
this vision, and it still
took years to see
m y s e l f perpetuating
                              the problem. My vision is
                              so bad, for a long time
                              I couldn't see "Not All
                              Men" as "All Lives Matter"—

failed to acknowledge the damage
that can cause. Failed to make the connection
again.

I now understand where I lie in this poem,
that shrapnel is a seed, and masculinity is a metal.

I was the coke can, once standing by
watching the chaos, failing to realize
that I became just another part the problem.

[KANYE 3:20]

"Heyyyyy, Mama"

My mom was the most incredible photographer. I remember thinking as a kid that she could have been more famous than anybody I had ever known. In my eyes, she already was. Every time I looked down her lens, this came to mind. But she chased parenthood instead of fame, and the photos of hers that live brightest in my memory are the ones that captured my most thoroughly embarrassing moments.

There's one day I remember in particular. I couldn't have been older than five at the time. It was fall; I've always thought fall in Michigan is the perfect smell. I think it's the combination of rain, leaves spiraling away from trees, and the breeze being just strong enough to wander into rolled down windows and fall delicately in your nostrils.

I'm certain our red Geo Metro had more miles on it from riding together, windows down and music up, than it did from my mother's hours of commuting to and from any one of her numerous jobs. Her three jobs kept her nomadically crisscrossing the state, a single mother single-handedly working to make my childhood shine like her smile when focusing on what she loved. She traveled more times than I did in basketball, even before she taught me to shoot one. Despite the fact that that car was her work vehicle, I laid claim to it; doglike, marking my territory on the dashboard with a Stretch Armstrong doll. When we'd go on our adventures together, the doll would bake in the sun, appearance changing detail—an action figure, contortionist limbs reaching for the windshield with skin melting to the vinyl painted blue by the sun visor. Plastic insides melting the way wax does when you forget to put out the candle. But I did forget; I forgot that there was anywhere else in the world but here.

We would always grab a random something that fit our escapades the way a perfect hoodie seems to always be what the doctor ordered; something like McDonalds strawberry shakes—those were my Grandfather's favorite, so of course they were mine—a funny hat from Meijer, or a new cassette tape. On this particular day she had outdone herself. At Family Dollar, she picked out these wild black-framed glasses. They were connected to a large white nose with a squirly black mustache, and even came with a complementary plastic cigar.

She told me it was the face of somebody famous, but I remember recognizing my Grandad's features in the packaging. That same wispy mustache that tickled my nose when he went in for a kiss, and his less-than-spectacular bottom shelf silver-framed glasses that made me not so ashamed of having my own. So, I put them right over my frames rocking my six eyes, nylon facial hair, and big schnoz while puffing my plastic cigar with pride!

That day, as we drove to places that didn't matter with destinations that weren't planned, my eyes were wide and endless. I was only focused on my pilot to the left, her hands on a weathered leather steering wheel, and the very real possibility that I could truly be anything in the world if I worked hard enough and dreamed larger than life. If a boy from a halfway house littered with memories of a father that would never be could upgrade to a double wide after enough years of his mother breaking her back that I could now bask in amazement at her reflection in her master bathroom mirror as she prepared for her workday where she made this all possible, then where was the limit? It surely wasn't the sky, or my imagination; and the limitation surely wasn't my own face.

I gazed out through those dollar store spectacles that revolved around my own with eyes of a child that believed he could be anything. Just listening to Smokey Robinson's "Cruisin'," mom snapping pictures on her 35mm, smiling like she had never been more proud. Me just wanting to be more like everyone I had ever loved, imitate every bit of positivity I have ever seen, bellowing:

"And if you want it you got it forevaaaah!"

I remember I kept saying, "What's happening, suckas?" on repeat, and I remember her saying suckas was the right thing to say with this new face, though now I know the face was Charlie Chaplin (though I think she thought it was a gangster like Al Capone).

That day, I didn't know anything was incorrect, because in my life there was nothing that had ever felt more right. So, I chose to be present. I always did, and now I fear holding onto that innocence after the world has tried to steal it so viciously from my hands.

But this was before people entered my life that would change me forever; before molestation, or abuse, or the substances that would work as an excuse to behavior that I years later would still not have the grace to unburden myself of.

So, in all of my temporary innocence that day I asked her questions about topics that most truly honest parents dread answering. Questions like "Mom, who is God really?" and "Where do babies come from?" Sunshine caressing my skin, and melting Mr. Armstrong's as he, like me, became one with the humming the cars engine.

I think there is something truly profound about how even as just a child I could put on something that resembles my grandfather, see a father figure in the reflection in the visor mirror, and it spiraled my adolescent mind into arriving at this very moment like some divine inception.

I now understand that youth find security in representation, that a single dollar can brighten a day enough to not notice your favorite toy ruining your mother's dashboard by melting into nothing; like your insecurities in those moments when your high top fade was enchanted with the autumn breeze as your head hung out the window without fear of hitting the ground, and, like Armstrong, becoming one with the blackness.

"Baby let's cruise, away from hereeee,
Don't be confused, the way is clearrrr!"

I miss learning to be that free, letting myself hang out of the window, not yet even scared of death or knowing the meaning of the word.

I still don't understand the God part, though; how people say all of this could come from a single man, when everything around us was made by birth or rebirth.

She said, "Babies come from women, you came from me".

My joy, security, confidence, shoot even my very being was made by an incredible, dynamic, remarkable woman. It wasn't until man came into the picture—or didn't—that I understood what devastation was or the definition of the word destruction.

To think some people believe that Eve came from the rib of a man. They even say before that God, well *He* created it all. My momma taught me better, and now I believe in everything you can read above. Even myself.

Suckas.

[MAN VS. THE MACHINE]

      The story of his battle is a tall tale
I hear the oppressors doubted him.
          Thought their creation was foolproof.
The tales say
     he could drive a spike with his brawn; not steel, flesh;
                     faster than any man in the nation.

They say that his freedom was the prize of the wager,
     that the media bellowed:

        John Henry Vs. The Machine!

January 2016,
     a coworker exclaims: Bruh, they always
          want to keep the Black man down!

They systematically slander our names
     before we got one foot in the grave
          even when the other is taking strides for change

    MLK? An adulterer.
    Michael Jackson? A pedophile.
    And now Bill Cosby is a rapist!
       All while my nigga is about to buy NBC?! Tell me:

Why would you wait twenty-plus years to vocalize
                    your sexual assault?

     (Shit, Quaaludes were in, it was the seventies!)

He followed it up with a: "Bro, I was raised
     by a single mother struggling.
          So trust, I would never

think ill upon a woman.
I grew up
watching this man father
a nation of kids without one. I would
never doubt em'!"

I decided to put a wager against his privilege.
Turned his masculinity into poker chips, became studious
of his face, readily awaiting signs for a bluff.

I asked: So, out of curiosity, if you
were sexually assaulted tonight;
raped,
molested,
taken advantage of in a way that as a person
—naw as a "man"—
made you feel... anything less than such;
who would you tell?"

The cards played won me a timid: No one.
Well maybe... my best friend.
Maybe.

A response that would remind me I am still not truly
all in. I am gambling
scared, afraid to show my real hand.

And you can't win that way. Not with the pot
this high... not
when the stakes are misogyny, privilege, and teaching another man
about his flawed perspective.

The story of his battle is a tall tale.

They say spikes were used; that his freedom
was the prize of their wager.
You could hear people bellow:

Bill Cosby Vs. The Machine!

It was summer, July, I was not
                        even nine. In my mother's mind
                                at the time,
He was a father figure,
        a role model,
                a *real* man.

I had never planned
      on taking a shower with one,
            but we were camping.

Apparently, young boys should shower with their *"fathers"*
      here. Lord knows
            in a community bathroom one might wander
            or be abducted
            or victimized by a stranger.

But not I, not
    by a stranger.

How lucky of me.
I had an adult there for *protection*,
And while camping, show me how *it*
                        was done.

It. What a clown
      must I have been, not understanding
      what was in front of me. To not tell
      my mother, and face *it*.

                "You have to make   *it*   quick."

It was erect.   He asked with a grin: Have you ever seen
                                                      anything like it?

　　　　　　　　　　He asked me
　　　　　　　　if
　　　　　　I
would...
　　　　　　　　I thou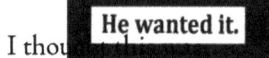
natural, a necessary part of becoming
　　　　　　　　　　　　　　a man.

After nearly 20 years, I haven't uttered
　　　a word of this to anyone, I haven't even
　　　　　　　　　　considered it. No one. Not even
　　　　　　　　　　　　　　　　　　　　maybe...
　　　　　　　　　　　　　　　　　　　　a best-friend

　　　　The story of *this* battle is *not* a tall tale.

I hear the oppressors doubting us.
　　　　But until people know they are able, safe, encouraged
　　　　　　　　　　　　to vocalize their assailants

　　the media will bellow:

If they allow themselves in the situation, they wanted it!

If they don't tell anyone, they wanted it!

I just want the safe memories
　　　　of my childhood back
　　　　before he entered it. But that will never happen...

　　　　　　　He wanted it.

2 / CHRYSALIS

SANTANA 4:18

"The fragrance of the lord on me—Purp N' Tommy. No
'Oochie Wally—I'm Harlem-raised
from broke to 'Paid in Full' word Killa Cam,
we the gospel to the East as Detroit is to Dilla fam—
from flashin' on the tele in the UK—to wood grain on the Yukon—
          we show 'em freedom's possible, that you can end
                with chains, a range, an' Franklins
                    and start from coupons."

*To the past versions of myself,
I had to honor you. It wasn't personal.
But the only way we can ever truly grow
is by finding that sacred space where you
can birth yourself from the birth, and manifest in
what was even before you knew what you can become.
And some times, you'll share while doing it.
Sometimes, you might think you'll grow. Still still destroy yourself.*

[KEHINDE]

Inspired by Kehinde Wiley's "Design for a Stained Glass Window with Wild Man"

When staring at this painting, I am reminded:

so many of us were never encouraged to dream—
that a Gold accent can be draped around us, fresh as an "04 Welcome to the Roc"
    chain—
that even without being a Diplomat we are destined to shine.

I see him relaxed, reclined
                  a co-pilot with his sneakers
          peekin' out the passenger; same
as any one of us at the time.

Working to cash out, glow out
               and now blow out stock speakers; just tryin' to shine.
               Bass maxed out
                     treble turned down
                          'fore we ever knew
                    we were missing *The Sound*.

      I roll with a gang of gangs,
      ho hang and bang,
      Animals, orangutans. Chanting:
                  Dipset—Dipset—Dipset

I coulda sworn I knew 'em—
            'fore I knew I didn't.
Loose 59Fifty, Easter Forces with the pastel patent, polo
      with a tall tee, and a miracle to match it—for too long I haven't seen
    this as magic.

Is that not Amerikkka's grand finale? Its greatest masterpiece?
    We play necromancer with the toe-tagged
        erect tombs out of hashtags, use shirts
        as memorials.
            The irony between cotton
            and a "Free Gucci, Assata, or
            a R.I.P" t-shirt
        is a metaphor
        I haven't yet mastered.

But here we are, in a museum on display,

basking in the work it takes
to bring us to *life*—
    when staring at this painting
I see that I was never encouraged to dream. That even if this boy is gone he lives.
        At least here; if not only here,
        flowers all around 'em while still above ground. To been seen
            cuffed
                without shackles. That is a *True Religion*.

Still vibrant and visible. This picture is:

    Javon going hard body to the lane,
        on Nike Court, when the surface was as teal as the seas
            we only saw in books

    Aaron's pull-up—   every time, net exploding as we turned
        firework on the sideline

    Kyle's pull-up—   every time, as our student section
        became a roar, before we felt
            like anything more than prey

    Kyron's pull-up—   every time, before fist fights
        landed more than shots

                        on double rims
This poem is me
being reminded we
      are more than *just* sports

every time. This work of art is:

    Jamaal's laugh
        after cookin' you

    my brother Keenan's voice
        on some Isley-Brothers-meet-D'Angelo type shit

    Darian's crossover
        in the day of And1 mixtapes
            with a touch of "Hot Sauce" added on with finesse

    Foster's new suit
        for each event, dripping 90's,
            like candy paint

    Martel's locks
        blowing in the wind, flying down Fulton Street
            on two wheels, no need for a destination

    Julius standing
        on a speaker at The Pyramid Scheme
            microphone in hand, not a care but a cadence—
                spraying water like a dragon, spitting bars like the gospel

    Kyontae: creatively uncontrollable
        brain untamed, hair a flame, mane
            out and dreaming...

This picture is my poems
This picture is my poems

this picture is...

All we have ever had   and always wanted.

The opportunity to be ourselves   without judgment

Celebrated for once

for being.

Just being.

⋮

To:

Darion, Samar, Foster, Julius, Martel, and Kyontae...

I love you.
Thank you for being amazing men, fathers, brothers, and sons.
Thank you for being Black and bold, and free.
Thank you for loving me, inspiring me, and glowing how only yall can.

[PARALLEL SYSTEMS]

My first experience in jail:

it took roughly 24 hours before I stared at the man who would decide my fate through a flat screen television in the corner of the room;

to this day I don't understand why they upgraded to LED TVs. I'm going to trust it was for energy efficiency.

Efficiency:

the way they move assumed felons; "troublemakers" "convicts" "law breakers" vomit, as well as brown paper bags containing *lunch* or *breakfast* (I use those words loosely) in order to keep the cells ready for fresh meat.

Fresh meat:

It is an industry standard in SLAUGHTER- houses to hang the carcasses for ten to fourteen days after SLAUGHTER.

I could never imagine laying lifeless in a jail cell for any amount of time. Body being refrigerated by central air,

concrete and cold hearts.

For Kalief Browder:

it started as adventures with friends, and ended

with people in power trying to lose him in a system made for us to lose.

For Sandra Bland:

> it started over a traffic signal. It progressed
> to a man very unnecessarily striking
> a woman.

Both continued with a symphony of screams—

> there was no brass section though,
> not where the eyes could see.

Only the cameras

> only the eyes

of the perpetrators that put lighting into them

> containing as much compassion as the machines

capturing the atrocities and

> working to open up space for more.

But with Sandy we could actually hear:

> the strings—
> vocal cords screeching

You can't just slam my head on the ground.

> I have epilepsy—

Finally the brass chimes in:

> "Good."

[RUBIK'S CUBE SHININ']

My criminal history is a Rubik's Cube
That hangs—Jesus-piece—on my neck.

Remnants of Cuban Linx in my ears,
Diamond- and star-studded dreams

That sit adjacent to my throat.
I doubt I'll ever complete it.

But as a fellow unfinished puzzle,
I'm not ashamed of the stories it tells.

I find myself focusing on the blue
And white.   I think it's funny

how PTSD shimmers brighter when the light
hits it and sings like a guilty verdict.

WAITING TO BE JUDGED

If not blackness,
        then what   is the text   on this page?
                      Science says: Black
                              is the *absence*
              of stimulation to the eye
      I have to disagree cuz
          how *stimulating* one must be
              to automatically be seen
as:
      Thief
          undeserving of equality
              Target
                not smart enough,
                      "I bet they quick though"—
                Rapper

Society says: Black is absence

so
      Dad must have truly been, cause I ain't seen 'em.   (REWIND)
      Dad must have truly been, cause I ain't seen em.

"Black is absence"
              (society says)
                        Rapper
                "I bet he's quick though"
              not smart enough
            Target
        undeserving of equality,
    Thief
              to automatically be seen

as

    how stimulating one must be

                                            I have to disagree, cuz.

"Black is the *absence* of stimulation to the eye"

                                            (science says)

Then what is the text   on this page
                                if not blackness,
                                    waiting to be judged.

[UPDATED DEFINITION I][1]

Racism (noun) rac·ism (rā-si-zəm):

The institutional bias created towards people of color caused by centuries of social rhetoric, oppression, and mistreatment that often allows false connections between a person's character and their skin color, perpetuating mistreatment. Racism often occurs when a person uses their own lived experience, anecdotal evidence, or the passing of time to invalidate the lived experiences of large populations of people, or to justify society's continued mistreatment of those people.[2]

Contrary to popular belief, racism does not necessarily arise out of hate. Rather, it can be involuntary and inherent, owing to socialization and the programming of supremacy through a failure to dismantle or address pre-existing power structures.

For further explanation see:

Redlining, gentrification, the three-fifths compromise, the convict lease system, the school-to-prison pipeline, 1930's Lending Maps, school segregation, housing segregation, and the way black history is taught in our European based education system.

---

[1] This definition has been made due to the vague definition in outdated dictionaries used as a scapegoat and justification of "Reverse Racism".

[2] Drawn from a definition of racism by Kate Pillsbury of The Crane Wives.

[WHEN THE GUN WEARS BLOOD; WHERE DO I PLACE MY FEAR]

He never just doesn't show.
    But when he didn't appear,
        I wore fear the way brown friends do
        when their family doesn't arrive.
        You litter your mind with "what if's"
wonder if America did what it does best:
made another black boy vanish, fed him to God.

My mind asks me if he is now the antonym
    of a nativity scene? Another recreation
        of a young black man lookin' Jesus in the news?
    It responds with: you know how rural white folks love
their nativity scenes.

Momma taught me
    to Google names before I worry to much.
        But when their name actually pops up,
        That is when the terror tucks
            in your sanity, and fury blooms
        sadness, fear, and Machiavelli from where
    a mason played Moses with the concrete.
I tell myself:

Don't read the comment section
Don't read the comment section

    Stick to the facts.
    Stick to the facts.

26 ARRESTED/FELONY GUN POSSESSION/THE WEAPON WAS FOUND IN HIS BACKSEAT/THEY SAW IT WALKING UP/ HE PUT HIS HANDS ON THE STEERING WHEEL/HIS CRIMSON

LITTERED THE PISTOL GRIP
But my mind continues to sprint.

MUST HAVE HELD IT SO TIGHT HE LEAKED FEAR OUT OF
HIS PALMS AS HE PRAYED TO GOD/AT LEAST HE WASN'T
CRUCIFIED/AT LEAST I DON'T HAVE TO CONNECT HIS NAME
TO PRAYER

Don't read the comment section
Don't read the comment section

I read the comment section.

HE IS A MURDERER/HANG HIM/JUST ANOTHER ONE DOING
WHAT THEY DO BEST/THERE HAS TO BE MORE TO THIS
STORY/I BET THEY FIND A BODY

At least it wasn't his—

Continue to read the comment section.

WHY WAS THE BLOOD ON HIS HAND/IT WAS PROBABLY
KETCHUP/DEATH PENALTY

Damn it—

Why did I read the comment section? Where do I set my fear?

Over here?
    Over there?
On the floor,
    with the gun?

[That Mourning]
[THAT MOURNING]

I started off that mourning
the same way I would start any other day:
scrolling through Facebook endlessly,
the same way I approach the refrigerator again
and again; as if I will find something new
that I hadn't seen the last twenty-seven times I looked.
I thought to myself: *put your stupid phone away, go back to sleep, because tomorrow
you have to nurture*
the young minds of Kelloggsville into fruition.

I rolled over...
but I kept scrolling, eagerly reopening
that refrigerator door. And it hit me
the way the smell of year-old forgotten leftovers
of Thanksgiving-past would.

A WZZM Channel 13 News headline read:
"Kelloggsville Teenager Gunned Down While Exiting the Bus"

I—not even a person
of faith—selfishly
started to pray.

    "Dear God: please...
    don't let it be one of our kids."

Hours later I continued to pray; this time
over a pew of porcelain, palms clasping the sides
for life. Yet I was familiar
with this position:

head lowered, eyes closed
head hung-over. Spewing out guilt
as if I would be hung—
over.
Until my eyes collide with another headline...
"FIRST YEAR Student Slain During Murder/Robbery"

Quickly realizing it had been a year since I was there.
I selfishly thanked God
as any *temporary* Christian would.

Until I started to see: comment after comment
branding this young boy's skin
the way slave masters would.

Posting pictures of him in a hoodie
while labeling him as a "Gangsta" due to his attire,
or posing with his friends.

Painting him in what they saw
as the only *true* shade of Black
with a brush made of the phrases:
He clearly had it coming
He was no saint
and *What did you expect?*

before the body was even cold enough to be in the ground.

As if young white suburban kids
aren't falling into the new fad of "Squad Pics"
by the thousands;
but when slain, you don't see little Ryan on the news
throwing up signs with his crew—
he is draped in a graduation gown.

While our young black
KIDS
children = Babies
Are falling
Unarmed
in the street
Then are dressed
As MONSTERS
by
The MEDIA

While our young black kids
are falling
            unarmed
                        in the street,
then are dressed as monsters by the media.
This is a peer of our students.
This is so near to *our* students.
But it is *all* near *our* students.

I walked into class later that day, assuming
that many teens in this community
failed to realize how this tragedy will plague them.

Minutes later, I was reborn over harsh truth.
A star pupil uttering:

    "That was my ex-boyfriend.
    Today, I wrote a poem for him."

A teacher fumbling over the fact that one of the murderers was a student in our school last year.

I badly wanted to open their eyes to the fact
    that police would now see more of us as violent,
    due to the rash actions of their peers—

that brown eyes quickly turn to bulls-eyes from pupils of blue and whites singing

    "Ring around the—
    Niggas you shouldn't have gotten so
    goddamn loud
    during the memorial!"

I stomached that respectability bullshit,
once again feeling nauseous,

finally realizing that it is time
to mourn, failing to realize that

every morn I myself scroll
and scroll, desensitized to the now-constant headlines,
failing to realize how hard we worked for this.
Not long ago, slain Black lives
didn't even make plain black text
appearing of much less relevance.

So many are becoming used to seeing those headlines... until it hits close to home.

Later that night I crafted our assignment for the following week: Write about why you will NEVER GET USED TO THIS.

Do it in plain black text, and let's give
those people in the news comment section
something to talk about.

[UPDATED DEFINITION II]

Reverse Racism (noun) re·verse rac·ism (ri-ˈvərs ˈrā-si-zəm):

[WHEN I DIE]

If I am murdered by: a police officer/a bouncer/a neighborhood watch official/ an individual just "standing their ground"/or at random

and I am described as *disgruntled/angry/or impossible to handle*

DO NOT
hold a candlelight vigil
in hopes that the flames
will be seen from the heavens—
                due to my past I more than likely will
                not end up there.

DO NOT
let anyone read poetry
about how unforgivable this is
while not holding the city accountable,
or intending on doing anything more than just gathering.

DO NOT
let those I love hold hands with the people who wanted me gone long ago.

DO NOT
let those who have said words behind closed doors say words when I can not.

DO NOT
appear to be leaves
once full of life
now piling on top of one another for one's enjoyment—
                I loved the fall, but this is not the way I want to celebrate my
                final one.
          Litter the city/with organic fury/that will dissolve back to the earth/like rose petals/or embers from Molotov Cocktails.

DO NOT
let #BlackLivesMatterGR pretend to give a flying FUCK about my black ass.

DO NOT
let the mayor give words of wisdom while hiding blindly
from the wrath that should ensue.

BURN THIS MOTHER FUCKER DOWN.
I want the city to be the candle.
I want all of the one-percenters' investments
to be the wax I see melting
from the afterlife.

DO NOT
let this incident go unpunished
or those saying *I just don't see why they would wreak havoc
on their own community... seems counterproductive*
wave their tongues, confederate.
This city has never been "ours," they show us this daily.
As we can't afford neighborhoods that have historically always been our own.
You pull out the rug, replace it while we are in the air, mid-tumble, and expect us
to land on our feet?

This catastrophe was not a hug of acceptance.
It was not a handshake, it was not meant
to be parted with so quickly.

DO NOT
post about me for a week like Sandra/Alton/or Trayvon
and pretend that it is activism—
pretend that you have done "all you can"
from the comfort of your own home
from the safety of your cell phone,
and the security of your privilege
safety-pinned to your overpriced jacket

(when I was rewarded neither of the above).

DO NOT
let the media outlets that
DID NOT publish the positive stories while I was alive
chose to misinterpret what I was saying during my existence
or those that were too scared to defend me while I was breathing pretend to care.

DO NOT
let my mother or girlfriend speak at this time.
    They are the empathetic ones
        and far too patient to convey what I would have liked to at this
        moment.

Do NOT
let Jesse Jackson in that motherfucker either.

PLEASE
call people the
FUCK OUT.

Do not
let people say "He was a saint"
or "The future" because clearly I was destined to end here…

I promise the future will be brighter with the youth carrying the torch.

DO NOT
let once-friends be heard when they try to utter words of kindness,
ex-peers say they "knew me well"
ex-co-workers say "they enjoyed working with me"

        I understand that I am a vessel for change.

Nobody praises the spacecraft when it collides into the earth after its voyage
    but it will burn bright and hot just the same.

Spread my ashes in the fire
        so that they can rebuild atop my body
and if gentrification eats away at what grows from the soil
        eradicate the vermin
and try again.

[BACK IN THE DAY]

when I was really, *really* young
I remember telling all of the other kids at school
my dad was a *superhero*
and that he was too busy
saving everyone else
to have any time
for me.

As I grew older, I started to refer to him
as Santa Claus—a man of folklore
and unfathomable presence
who only really comes upon the mind
once or twice a year when its cold,
and you are entertaining
the thought of warmth.

        Feeling whole
        instead of mason-jar-with-firefly—
        my empty spaces always light up
        when I'm the darkest.

Today, for what seems like
the hundredth time, I listened
to my biological father whisper me bittersweet
nothings via a cassette tape,
delivered in an envelope
postmarked 1988.

        A symphony of *Not Shits*
        Can't Dos, Won't Dos, Should Haves,
        and *Will Nevers*—twenty glorious minutes
        of why he can't and won't ever be
        in my life. How thoughtful of him!

He should have titled it:

Why You Don't Have a Dad,
sealed it with a kiss, or his cologne,
or some sweet lovey-dovey movie shit,
instead of getting my fucking middle name wrong
on the outro; a wholehearted middle-finger-post-sucker-punch
below the belt.
Ya know what, fuck it—

let's throw in a Mike Tyson, biting-through-my-cartilage
cheap shot metaphor
in this part right
here.

Nahhhh.
We'll save the fancy word play
and beautiful imagery
for a poem *not* about him.

> This isn't that poem.
> This won't be his poem.
> I will not give him something
> to be proud of.

Why do you think I live my life like this?
Two parts self abuse.
Seven parts fearful of success.
One part neglect.
No parts self-love, though.

I'm not going to pick up where he decided to leave off,
I'll leave it there: on the shelf with the cape
he never chose to wear, in the closet
with the other childish fantasies.

Two weeks ago, I saw God
from the back of a Lexus Coupe.
He looked like a coked-out felon, smelled
like fear and recovery.

He chose to total the car
going a hundred and twenty miles an hour,
and made me realize that I am only a human.
He had my life in his hands,
clearly forgetful of my existence,
disregarding that he had souls in the back seat.

> Tried to turn a Fable
> into an anecdote.

I climbed out of a totaled car
kissing the ground the way the police like us to.

> Us, Black. Thanks, Dad.
> I appreciate the gift of life.

My life
keeps spiraling out of control.
I bet he's proud.

> I am a hurricane of heartbreak and ugly shit.
> *What am I doing here?*—
> *How did I get here?*—
> is what I ask myself most nights,
> mouth tasting like "well something"
>
> because, well...I had to use something
> to make myself feel better
> before I use someone.

I get that from him.

[Handwritten note: Note: I wonder if I can include actual audio of the tapes?]

I always rewind and play back
the part where he talks about his love life.
"Son, my son, I've never been any good
at relationships, you can ask your mother this
one day."

I have a secret...
I never asked her.
I never wanted to know.

But you know what's the worst part?
He ended it with a poem. Before he ever knew
what I would be most passionate about.
He ended it with a poem.

For *months*, I've hated poetry.
I would hear him speak at open mics,
and watched him turn my safe haven
into a battleground of self-discovery.

I played hopscotch on a minefield of my vices
hoping I would land in them
and not wake up to another day
of picking up pieces
of myself.

Back in the day
when I was really, really young

I wasn't broken.
I'm hoping I can find that boy again.
I will shower him in comic books and cartoons.
I will tell him not to look for his father here.

I will tell him one day he can be a hero—
at least, to someone.

[handwritten annotations: This last line, tattoo it on your bones. And when you feel low, Remind yourself You-can-fly.]

[THE FRAYED EDGES OF MY BLACK CARD]

Proper English doesn't fit in my wallet anymore. It used to have a place
next to the clementine ribbon   (the one that always makes me cry my ugly
authentic cry from stories of sobriety)the one that was placed in my palm
with a whisper and a smile. It took up the space neighboring my "black card"
but it always (*always*) caused its edges   to fray and split   so   I   think
it is time to
throw it away. It's too loud, and stands in like conformity. I only want
                        capitalism and sad stories in my wallet. Stuff that smells of
freedom, and the present tense. I think I kept it in my soul too long during the time
warrants hung over my head like death, stale cigarette smoke, and ganja cologne.
    I always wrote new numbersof old flings on the back of it—people
who might bail me out when my walls began to close inwhen the law came, and I
needed a savior   like white Jesus, or the phrase   "Absolutely not officer"
"I had no idea there was a warrant for my arrest"
"I could have sworn I paid
my court fines sir"   when   "I ain't saying shit"   will get me the same result.
I just hope I'm alive to hold the ribbon tomorrow; it still smells
       like   the   pride   in   my   students'   eyes.

[LOST AND FOUND GOD]

Before then, I never really believed in two things:
God, and the ability to completely lose one's sanity.

When my mother called, she asked
when was the last time I talked to my grandfather.
Really *talked*... had to have been graduation. But I lied.
I replied, "It's been a while... probably a few months? Why?"

Hearing my mother cry was as common as an eclipse.
I could feel her tears on my cheeks through the phone
as the heat of the battery swallowed the water
drying the riverbeds on my face. But her sun couldn't hide that day.

She proceeded to say, "He's not doing so well...
I'm almost to Michigan, he's unresponsive;
Hospice is there, they are taking good care of him, I promise.
Can you make time to come say goodbye?"
"Can I make... time... No... No, yeah.
Yeah, I can. See you soon."

My knees gave out. Before I knew it, I was screaming for my best friend
at the top of my lungs, Mitch,
losing air with every bellow, MITCH! My sails
losing grasp of the wind. He wasn't there.

But I—
I knew this. I just needed someone.
I called my mother back. "I can't do it."
Before she hung up she said, "Hold it together, I'm on the way".

I paced through my house, smoking cigarettes
in pairs, double-fisting what escalated my once-father's demise, becoming sicker
with myself with every puff.
ENOUGH!

I couldn't let him see me like that.
So I ran to my room to freshen up.

And there it was... a card.
I thought to myself: *My mom let my friend
know before me...* Immediately filled with rage
and disgust I tore it open:

> *Marcel,*
> *We aren't as close as we used to be. But just know I'm SO proud of you,*
> *I can't wait to see the impact you have on the world.*
> *Love always,*
> *Grandpa*

A letter on my bed of rest
while he is on his bed of death...
what kind of sick fucking joke
is this? I ran into every room,

looking for a culprit
before I realized that I was two days home alone.

I reached for the phone
again. Hit one on the speed dial.

"Mom—"
"I'm almost there..."

"Why would you have them put the card
he gave me on graduation on my bed?"

"Hold on, I'm almost there.
I didn't, I promise."

The only words utterable were:
"I'm scared. Is he here?"

[SELF PORTRAIT OF THE CATERPILLAR AS HIS GRANDFATHER]

Whenever my family talks about my grandfather
    they always mention the drinking.
        I didn't sign up to play my elder's cameo,

yet here I stand, looking in the mirror
    Tupac shots deep into a fifth of (insert anything).
        It reads "proceed with caution" like subtitles
    on a TV screen.

Like I need closed captioning for my own reflection.
    I was born in the fall, but during his rise.
        "Marcel," my mother says, "you know he quit

when you and your cousin were born.
    He wanted to be better for you."
        Most times I can't even be better for me.

You can still find beer cans scattered across his property,
    hundreds of acres in Greenville, Michigan
        filled with tiny shimmering reminders under
    morning dew—

or do decades of leaves from so many falls now
    cover up the past? Meanwhile, on my front porch
        (on the west side of Grand Rapids) piles of cigarette ashes grow.

I remember being only thigh high, picking up these aluminum
    breadcrumbs and asking my uncle where they lead.
        Too young to understand that when tearing whole things

into little pieces, it isn't always done to find your way home.

There were too many people running away from their residence
        that found solace in those woods. Father's, Husbands, Brothers,
        Grandfathers,
            Bosses, sometimes all adding up to the same totem.

Over time yeast becomes hard. Croutons turn train tracks
        on foliage not edible enough to stomach.
            I still can't swallow the fact that one man

can be multiple. Natural Born Quitter
        that was quit on, that can't quit
            the shit that I need to. Irony.

My mom told how her father was an alcoholic;   Grand one
was too; before work she utters,
            "I can't imagine how it feels to hear

the one person you looked up to battled the same demons as you."

At times I think it's easier to swim
        in a half fifth and a pack
            than to go back to AA meetings where the only thing that they lack

is the booze. Smoking more squares in a circle
        than the Eastown house parties that sparked it all.
            I still don't fit it. I feel Incomplete Rubik's;

I'm losing grip,
        slipping, falling, and I
            can't get up.

[METABOLIZATION]

The butterfly

      is everything

           that the caterpillar

                          crammed

        inside itself,

          experienced,

          and didn't know

                          it had.

        What you are

           experiencing

        might be ugly

                          now,

     but one day

        you too will

evolve.

3 / TRANSFORMATION

It is now 2024 and I am now seeing that what I thought was "Transformation" was only a dream while I ate myself alive.

1 BODAK 6:12

"I don't wanna choose," you say—
decisions ain't always a commitment. "I don't wanna choose"
—bet I won't be mastered
by choice.

Note: The musicality needs to evolve! It needs to grow with the seasons, the same way the writing, views, and revelations have.

[MORE FLAVOR THAN A GOOD 'YO MOMMA' JOKE]

Your LaCroix liking friends are so bland,
    when they see it for sale in an online ad
they lick their screen to find their favorite flavor.

Your LaCroix liking friends are so tasteless,
    they think mayonnaise has a little bit too much spice.
Ohhh, it's making me sweat.

If your LaCroix drinking friends were vampires
    they would feed on H&M catalogues.

Your LaCroix drinking friends are the type to say
    "*Okurrt*" and "*Yaaaaaaas Queen*" to Beyoncé's "Lemonade"
with about the same level of flavor as Lemon La Croix.

Your LaCroix drinking friends likely invented the term
    "Eat the booty like groceries".

Your LaCroix drinking friends are prolly SO BIG
    They don't even have enough room
for the brown people in their neighborhood.

Your LaCroix liking friends are so boring they

    think
Roseanne is quality television
    think
Nike Monarchs are stylish shoes.

        (Love hot sauce, but only Cholula.)

Your LaCroix drinking boyfriend
    gives you oral sex
with Saran Wrap.

[Handwritten annotations: "TRUTH" / "I read this as a Comedy Monologue in an acting audition... I was so scared as I could have sworn at least one drank it."]

Your LaCroix drinking girlfriend
        thinks lip syncing "I wanna vacuum"
is synonymous with talking dirty.

Your LaCroix drinking boyfriend
        thinks his man bun is tasteful.

        thinks

identifying as feminist is deserving of a blowjob

        thinks

he has properly dissected his toxic masculinity

Your LaCroix drinking friends are trustworthy
        like the phrase *urban revitalization.*

        think

"everything doesn't always have to be about race"

        think

rappers wearing gold chains is tasteless

        think

a Jesus piece is more about capitalism
        than believing God could shine on them for once.

Are more Macy's mannequin than Eboney Patterson's
        dripping loud and black like a pastel orange church hat, or an Afro
Punk greatest outfit revival ceremony.

Your LaCroix drinking friends have yet to learn
        taste isn't always a factor

of flavor.

Love their food as diverse as a meal
        before the colonization of countries

The taste of a popsicle
        through a Trojan

Enjoy Cherry-
        flavored condoms.

The world is full of flavor,
        and some of yall choose Taylor Swift over Cardi B,

Dab in solidarity to Hip-Hop
        and have less swagger than George Bush's fingers
after sneaking candy to Michelle Obama.

But some of you prefer a drink to taste like something
        that was sitting in the room close to it.

In summation: if you are what you drink,
        y'all are corny.

NOTE:
Olipop and Poppi
are
absolute
Flame Emoji

[PLAYING, JUST FOR YOU]

Sometimes,
I see white

folk drag black
bodies through my news feed
giving it similar history
to Mississippi mud blood-
littered roads—phone screens morphing
into pickup trucks with General Lee-painted windows
and nooses hanging from the hitch
celebratorily towing limp
melanin like tin cans
"Just Married" to their beliefs
while self-righteousness proudly hangs
from their hands.

Sometimes,
I see them jump

on the necks of the
Jacqueline Dixons, Trayvon
Martins, Mariah Careys, Nick
Cannons, Rekia Boyds, Erykah
Badus, Drakes, Jussie
Smolletts, Cory
Bookers, Rihannas, or Kamala
Harrises with excitement,
entitlement and a smile.

Sometimes,
I see the nefarious

                                or guilty Cosbys
                            and Tygas get strung up
                          by pale hands and lugged
                      with excitement instead of allowing
                               these figures' own
                           people to do the bidding.

Yet for some
reason, regardless the deeds
of the flesh, I get sick from Caucasus elation
to rev engines and floor the gas ferrying
bodies through a sea of white presumption that was
never built for us.

                                    A brown trial
                                   is never a hearing
                                     to white ears.

Lately,
to put myself

                               at ease, I take
                         myself back to the days
                           before I noticed
                        they were starving to feast
                          on us. Ones centered
                      in lunchroom cyphers and hallway
                            freestyles. Where we used
                            black magic to morph
                      trash cans into bass drums, turned
                         cafeteria tables into snares.

Now,
when my feed grows stressor

                              from watching them feed
                                        on us, I pull out
                                       joy from my pocket
                                 in the form of the world's
                                    tiniest...beat machine.

                    Dum
              Dum Dum Dum Dum.
                    Dum
              Dum Dum Dum
         Dum Dum Dum Dum.
              Dum Dum Dum.

I fill
space the way the sound
of us did in high school, recreating
stripped-down versions of *Grindin'*
on loop that rattled through
the corridors of our campus
like a herd of bull.

                                              They assumed
                                            we were pushing
                                                 for malice.

Cause Pharell,
they've been doing just
that on repeat, while mounting us
where all eyes can see
since the day of news
stands instead of feeds.

                                         Hear ye, hear ye, read
                                                all about it!

Most times,
I rap the aggressive

                                            stuff I would love to say
                                            out loud in my own
                                            head like Issa Rae,
                                            which is to say
                                            I keep
                                      the responses to myself
                                    because I imagine they seem
                                    less threatening that way.

                   I feel like they want me to snap/
                   But expect me to be angry and black.

                   Got me looking crazy in the mirror
                   Hearin' Knuck if you buck,
                   Like boyyyy,
                   Boy better let them know,
                   They can get it on sight.

See,
I've been

                                            manhandled by white
                                          fragility since before
                                          I knew what the word
                                          'molestation' meant.

I've been fighting

                                          over slurs, micro-
                                          aggressions, and overt
                                          acts of racism way before
                                          my fists could clench rose

                              out of ivory and were labeled
                              dangerous and could be seen
                              labeled defensive.

So for now,
I may be seen

                              staying the way they
                              want me: quiet.
                              But I
                              refuse
                              to play dead. Be just
                              another rattling iron-filled
                              something dangling from someone's
                              bumper.

But, if I lose my joy

Though I
think my palms
are less likely to be crucified
if they are seen
wielding a tiny beat
pad instead of going
at the throats and thorns
of those trying to plant me.

                              I can't fit
                              even the world's smallest
                              beat machine in a pair of pants
                              that are full of my own
                              balled fists and bitten
                              tongues.

I will keep playing

But, if I lose
my joy *Just for you.*

                              :)

>   it is only a matter
>   of time before my patience
>   turns gunpowder to a temper
>   with the aim of Tubman's
>   musket.
>   So for now

I will keep playing

>   Dum
>   Dum Dum Dum Dum.
>   Dum
>   Dum Dum Dum
>   Dum Dum Dum Dum.
>   Dum Dum Dum.

Just for you.

[LOVE IS]

Her backhanded statements
land on my
chin with the grace
of a Robin on a street sign.
But
the intersection between bein' off balance
and love   is where God lives.

I have never been the religious type,
But I   swear to God,
              she could be one.
So I swear to her.

I swear every time she says:

"You've written poems about *every one* of your temporary-ass exes, but I don't hear a poem about the woman you say you want to marry?!"

Fuck!
But she
is
right.

I want to marry her.

For longer than I can remember, I played house
in women's imaginations.
Every relationship a Truth-or-Dare-me-to-leave

As honesty would never reside beneath the floorboards—
our foundations   never more than hot air.
My lovers   always baskets holding open
pieces.   Our heads balloon,
blooming to my words   fueling us to stay together.

My Love,

So much of my life after this book will be a tribute to you.

But she is wrong about one thing.

I did not write poems about *every* one of my exes!
Though because of you,   I wish I did.

    They say: "BAD Relationships make GREAT poetry."
But I have to disagree.

Because I've heard some really shitty (awful) love poems.

Hell I've written 'em.
Even memorized 'em.

They give my lemon of an engine just about as much comfort as the PTSD

but our hearts were never made to work correctly,
                        were they?

We are both machines built by workers
that never learned how to construct them right the first time.

We are reminded of this
                  every time we hit a pothole,
our pistons lock,   our engines seize,

and we look around for a healthy example
of how our engineers overcame
the same obstacles.

But we have no healthy relationships to compare ours to.

Every time someone makes a request for one of *their* poems—
I see it on page in my book—   or, God forbid
my agent thinks it would   "Play well in a college market"

[handwritten annotation: She really did hate when I read poems about my exes. As she should!]

I am reminded that there is no market for words about you.
There is only one for the dysfunctional shit.

No one wants to hear   about the nights
when your heartbeat   is the lullaby playing metronome
                to my grandmother's
voice.

The voice I remember from my childhood with only
"You Are My Sunshine" as a selection in the jukebox.

You give it that funky rhythm though the drunk kick
Boom   Boom   Boom   Boom

That deep pound, Op Knock   that stops the PTSD
            from crawling into nightmares.

But we aren't going to go there…

I don't want this to become just another
poem about my past
when I am now focusing on the future.

Head in the clouds   but no longer being fueled
                by hot air.

I once heard someone say that
"man was created in the image of God"

That nigga was a damn lie;
how else could I get so high
when experiencing you.

I *did not* write poems about every one of my exes—though at times I wish I did.

That way,   I could say
                              something cheesy like:

"That is because I always write about the past,
but it is now safe to say I know my future."

[WHAT A WONDERFUL WORLD]

> "I hear babies crying, I watch them grow.
> They'll learn much more, than I'll ever know.
> And I think to myself, what a wonderful world."
> —Louis Armstrong

As the warm rays of morning sun greet us
through the withered ivy-framed eyes of a Montessori classroom,
the teacher plays gardener to a jazz band of vivacious adolescent

seedlings in her middle school AP English class. As they tune their daily
    discretions
she plants them in a circle, interrupting teen gossip, and statements of
how terrible their lunch was with patience

met with abidance. Once all of them are
calm, ears ready, and voices prepared to chime over our sighs of relief
that they are—actually—calmed down... we start off

with an icebreaker: "I want everyone to compliment
the person on their left,
let's start with Sarah."

The fuse is lit. Its wick burns through
the first three young girls that sit beside each other every week
with ease, a dynamic explosion

of feminine energy that bounces off of white square cork ceiling tiles,
rattles windowpanes, and shakes
the DIY mason jar candles and paper lanterns

that make this room feel safer than everyone's childhood dream home.
You can hear the roar of smiles and see sparks of authenticity cut through
the shackles of competition

that society forces on the ankles of these young
women; these brilliant, vibrant, sharp humans destroying chains
with molten statements of: "I love your energy."

Another to Bri on her left: "I love that you aren't scared to be you!"
Another to Chontae: "You are the bravest person I know."
And positivity flows through the classroom like first rain in spring

falling upon parched ears. We watch confidence bloom, each smile a new
petal allowed to blossom, not plucked and discarded with an *I love me,
I love me not*—

Until the third girl gets
to a boy, says: "Victor, I love your smile...
and you always have the flyest shoes!"

His face blossoming, a grand finale of reds and whites,
teeth cheesin', cheeks a stoplight praying she runs it.
He says, "stooooop," but his smile says *proceed*.

But that boy turns to his left, and lo and behold, sees...
another *boy*. His grin fades.
Voice crackling in an off-key horn solo, he trumpets:

"I am *not* complimenting another guy...
That's... That's ga—" fists clenched so hard
his fingertips debated whether or not to breach

through his palms. "I don't like guys, I'm NOT..."
He pauses. Looks around. Lets out
a reluctant: "Well... I've just *never* done it before..."

Time after time, week after week, when we would meet during these workshops,
I'd feed them compliments
until they were full, and then fed them more.

Soul Food, every Thursday for lunch.
"Xavier, see you got a smile that'll make a puppy blush".
"Ryan, you are so passionate you make music listen to the sound of your voice".

and Victor, thank you for always teaching me—more than you'll ever know—
so that this cycle, at least in this class, would never again break because of a boy,
eager and willing to grow

who was just never taught that he could be
kind. One lesson at a time. And I hope they think
to themselves: what a wonderful world.

[THE STORIES THEY SHARE]

On Tuesdays,
I use poetry as a Trojan Horse
to teach the not-so-wide-eyed
about The Fair Housing movement.

The cause of their slumber could be
that talking about civil rights before the crack of dawn
is snooze-worthy at best—that before
lunchtime, I am more monotone
than high definition.

Or at 7:30 in the morning
when the sun hasn't even tucked in the moon yet
and my pupils haven't even wiped the sleep
tucked away in the corners of their window sills

    I fear waking them.

I feel less deserving of their attention
or priority treatment
than the stories they share
when woke.

    Freewrites of transient homelifes, unjust evictions, and constant noise.

I respect their lust for peace and slumber
so I let them.

One of my favorite students
dreams for at least the first twenty minutes of each class as I speak in an octave
not high enough
to reach his adolescence.

NOTE: Shout-out to foster and The Amazing People at The Fair Housing Center of West Michigan. Look up "Writing to right wrongs".

Ya see, I don't want to wake him up.
So I don't.

America has shown us
that when their eyes are open to infinity
it lusts for spreading the most vibrant
across the streets,
car seats, and hotel balconies.

That it yearns for us to teach them to speak

so that it can spread their everlasting sea
on the evening news—on repeat
on Facebook,
shared
on repeat
on Facebook.

As he dreams, I have nightmares
of sharpshooters that crave immortality
through destruction like the crescendo of a history book—

And I know they would put it on repeat.

Share his beautiful throat morphing Martins.

Magicianing his Adam's apple into a mouth-that-spits-out-lead
and calls it a murder's legacy—
before he can even have one.

Favorite student Number Two smacks
her gum with confidence, shows me
protective styles were made to defend her
money-maker mind: brilliant and
is going to be The First Black Female Whatever-She-Wants.

I am terrified of giving her more wealth, in fear
that their hunger of wanting to steal her
will grow.

Until I realize:
she could be praying in a church,
pulled over for a turn signal,
playing my heart strings in a symphony,
or be rattling off something brilliant in our classroom

    and they won't lust for her exit any less.

On Tuesdays,
we give them shields
to pair with tongues. I mean swords,
I mean I can't afford
to give them a weapon
when their phone can be seen as one.

I hear:
"So, my cousin wouldn't want to go to court

without a lawyer—so this is like
"1-800-Call-Sam"
but for unfair home shit?!"

    I reply: "Kinda, but it's not so black and white."

She always breezes through
with something elegant—chimes in:
"Because housing affects us all—it's an Everyone Issue right?"

Connects the stars, they make
universities out of constellations
drawing fine strokes
between redlining and quality of education.

As they learn to lead us north, I can't help but to wish them back to REM.

In week one, we learn about how Dr. King
ignited this movement.
We talk about his final speech,
"Somewhere I Read"—

> Somewhere I read that a young man once had a dream; grew into a man
> that had enough courage to be the dam to a nation.

And they Katrina'd him—intentionally blew through his levy.

Somewhere I read
that education was one of the only weapons
we have in a fight against inequality,

Somewhere I read
that teens are learning to stand,
even after bullets rip through their innocence.

One day I hope to read
that the ones we encourage to lead
feel safe enough to do so knowing
we will kick down our doors
even when the monsoon is at our doorstep.

> Open our windows, and let the hurricanes in
> knowing our young people are outside braving the storm.

My biggest fear is the older generation
not willing to even toss them an umbrella
much less their body as a sandbag to the chaos.

On Tuesday,
when our students finally feel
comfortable enough to rise

I will tell them somewhere I read:
April 3rd, 1968 in Memphis, Tennessee,
in spite of a severe storm warning
people came.

    Warn them that the world is full of unnatural disasters, show them;
    even nature doesn't match the power inside them.

And if anyone tries to stop them,
our bodies will be the only thing
we shutter around them, before any devil
even attempts to take a shot
that we will be damned
if we just sit inside and watch.

Forever

Adults,
We need to keep this energy...

[ROSEWOOD SONNET]

Righteous black magic, ritualistic worshiping of ancestors, flexing of spirits, exquisite collaboration of shamanistic
patience, and boar Bristol. Durag mimicking the vibrancy
of Maasai warriors in Kenya, Muhammad Ali
in a velour jumpsuit, or Cam'ron in Purple Mink. Nothing
but genes, and confidence catcalling praise from peers
as soon as the headdress parts like clouds on someone's sun and literally changes definition, like a smooth entendre—
I watch the sun rise in the moment where the upper rim of the horizon appears into morning. And when the other stars notice, the roar of "damn" echoes through the wards
of this classroom. Praise Milly rocking on tongues and off tongues and tabletops only stopping for an "I see you". Watching these black boys smile and feel wholly themselves—this is what I love for every Thursday.

Pete W,
You are and will forever be a legend.

OHHS,
To the students, teachers, staff, and alumni of Ottawa Hills High School. You are the seasoning to Grand Rapids. The flavor. The legacy. The Magic. Do not get smaller. Make the world grow to you!

[TERRIFYING TRUTHS]

Today I'm meditating on a terrifying truth:
                              there are more suicides at the Golden Gate Bridge
than any other single place in our country.

More people travel there to end their story: flesh coated
                              iron, and someone's favorite heartbeat
venture to this location from all across this trauma-ridden sphere

to crash through one of the world's largest mirrors. The bay, this
                              structure; an undeniable magnet, it pulls matter
from all corners of the globe. Drags blood out of its home—

attracts with the promise of wind rushing around you, cradling you
                              vigorously as every frantic last breath
pushes back at nature like a nonviolent protest. A coin toss,

enticing you with one final look at yourself in the reflective
                              face of the ocean. Fact: I have contemplated taking
my own life a thousand times. But there are two

reasons I have never considered this Route 1 route:
                              1. Because I am terrified to
death of heights. Even the thought of crossing bridges

makes my palms secrete fear. And if I was to stand
                              at the edge of life, and had a heart attack
before I close this last chapter—that would be one

last thing I couldn't do right. And
                              2. Because I am sure that during that final
gaze into the water's truth, I would see all of my

abusers reflecting off the surface. I would be reminded of not only
how I got there, but of my own terrifying truth: that my face too may appear in someone else's final moments...

and that is something I deserve to live with.

THE UNITED STATES VS
THE COURT OF PUBLIC OPINION (TCOPO)

THE PEOPLE,
  Plaintiff,

Case Number 19-10888-CC Hon. Huey P Freeman

THE PEOPLE,
  Defendant,

Plaintiff lawyer info	Defendant lawyer info
John Doe (P5191925)	Jane Doe
Counsel for The People	Counsel for The People
Ingham County	Fulton County
Prosecutor's Office	Prosecutor's Office
3230 Alfred Ave	501 Auburn Ave
Lansing, MI 48906	Atlanta, GA 30312
555-555-5555	555-555-5555

MOTION FOR RELIEF FROM JUDGEMENT UNDER TCOPO 9.500

The Defendant, THE PEOPLE, through counsel, respectfully moves this Court to stop using its own judgement to oppress itself and grant the opportunity of oral argument for the people to be heard TCOPO 9.500 et seq., and states the following:

  1. You have the right to remain silent. *(Can not be incentivized unless you speak)*

(i) If self-proclaimed activists do not believe in rehabilitation, their mirrors will inform them that they are cogs in the same machine that incentives felons into repeat criminals, ensures they are unable to find housing, and launches their vessels into a job market Milky Way with no planet to call home.

2. Anything you say can and will be used against you in the court of public opinion.

(i) Speak wisely, with intent, and understand that nothing is off-limits. There is no statute of limitations on ignorance. Your lack of knowledge is not an excuse, you should have always known.

(ii) There is no minimum age exempt from punishment and no separate court for different offenses. We have not determined felonies, misdemeanors, or sentences for punishable offenses so the prosecuting populous will only request mandatory maximums.

3. You do NOT have the right to an attorney.

(i) There are no lawyers in the court of public opinion, but people have the right to cape for you at their own expense. When stepping into this wall-less justice system understand that what this courtroom lacks in concrete, pictures of old white people, and 'history' it makes up for with reach. As there are no 'barriers,' physical presence is irrelevant. So speak wisely, with intent, and understand that nothing is off limits.

Your family, children, significant other, pets, co-workers, and any/all other 'innocent until proven guilty' parties are considered guilty by association. They want you in court alone.

(ii) This forced isolation is not considered abuse, not seen as facilitating power and control over someone, and is not the same tactics the oppressive majority has always used to create the pipeline currently in place.

(iii) It is okay for you to be Kalief Browdered here. Prosecuted young, underrepresented, kept in the system regardless of following offenses, locked into isolation, and forgotten about.

(iv) If you are seen holding your tongue in hand while people stand for you, are being defensive, tasteless, or lack sincerity—individuals have the right to NOT stand with you while being questioned.

(v) If you are caught shielding your ears while being questioned, you will be found guilty in the court of public opinion.

4. You have the right to be called out for any and all toxic behavior.

(i) If toxic behavior is brought to light, you have the right to be left in the dark under Blacks v. Dolezal, 2016 or Spacey v. House of Cards, 2017. If toxic behavior is never remedied and continues to be perpetuated see The People V. R Kelly 2019.

5. You have a moral obligation to apologize.

(i) If an apology does not include what you did wrong, who you wronged, is vague, unauthentic, lacks sincerity, and is made to the public but NOT the person(s) you wronged, you have the right to be found guilty under People V. CK, 2017 or Minorities V. Law Enforcement Est. Forever.

(ii) If you think an apology relinquishes you of all guilt and continue to live like nothing happened you have the right to be dragged by the community.

(iii) If you expect combatants will apologize, or that this treatment relinquishes you of all guilt, you will be found guilty in the court of public opinion. When you have been forgiven by those you wronged—if you are forgiven—then you will wait to be arraigned... but don't hold your breath.

6. You have the right to make your life's work combating the injustices you have perpetuated.

(i) If this started before said issues were brought to the court of public opinion, and you have always been transparent about your wrongdoings, you will be given 1 gold star. A gold star is not to be confused as a "pass".

(ii) If you are seen wanting praise for rehabilitative work, NOT for doing the work because it is the right thing to do—you can take your ass back to jail. (Do not pass go, do not collect stipends or honorariums.)

(iii) You have the right to restorative justice—NOT to be confused with the right to be forgiven.

(iv) The New World is a planet rooted in solutions, rooted in vulnerability expanding to trees mimicking accountability, you have the right to breathe oxygen only as clear as the carbons you emit into our solar system.

Inhale, exhale. Ask yourself: are you polluting, or enhancing our air? Do you understand each of these rights as I have explained them to you?

    ____ Yes
    ____ Yes

Having these rights in mind, do you wish to speak to us now?

    ____ Yes
    ____ Yes

[FALL ON GOLD]

November on Gold Street.

Blocks away from *The Bitter End*
of a neighborhood divided.
The city doesn't even try to hide it.

But they keep trying to test me.

    But   they keep trying   to   test me.

The Little Caesar's around the corner says:
"We no longer serve Pepperoni Cheese Bread"
as if they stopped stocking pepperoni...
or Cheese Bread...

I'm not going to lie, y'all,
this might be the straw that broke the camel's back
but I smoke American Spirit; a pack a day *rate*   *without a market*
keeping the stress of rent-raising away.
                                              in sight.

    They are charging market rate
    without a market   in sight.

We don't need a Meijer or Target down the street—
we are wearing bulls-eyes already.
Bask   in that for a while.
They are gunning for our exit; drive by
but not at night, there are no street lights.
You won't be able to witness.

    Bask   in that for a while.

My neighbor tells me
the woman that used to live here had
"one hell of a green thumb."

Too bad   passion   didn't pay the bills.

The roses she planted
before her eviction
tell me *good morning* from my shady porch.
They wave hello, tip their crimson
fall floppy hat at me through gravel stones
showing me she *was* one hell of a botanist. ~~Longer than the stories~~

    ~~Too~~ bad   passion   didn't pay the bills.

I wonder if he will tell
the next tenants that I was
"one hell of a writer".

I wonder if the words of encouragement
that I and my girlfriend
litter on their children's minds
will last larger than the value of our home—

    Longer   than the stories ~~of jade~~ ~~of~~ ~~jade~~ digits. *(d.g.'s.)*

The Ghost of Tenants Past
still haunts our entryway.

I wonder if our landlord will paint
over the hieroglyphics left by *her* children,
or if they will stay as a reminder
that we are only as good as the green
in our pockets, not the crayon-coated phrase
that greets you when entering our home.

The voice of this pre-pubescent child bellows
pipe organ—and brings me to church
every time I go to leave.
I imagine fingers still embracing Crayola keys...
It reads: *Asshole*.

I assume this message was written
to the people that asked them to go,
those remodeling their home
the same way they are restructuring
the community
for higher income.

It is November on Gold Street.

In July, there was a ranch home behind us.
There is now a concrete slab
where a home once stood,
Yet here, I hear, we have
an issue with lack of housing...
Irony.

Two doors down from me
a shiny new blue door
secures the nicest residence on the street.
A home erected quicker than my morals.

A home erected quicker than my morals.

Every Friday night
But I already know they want us to leave.
when they party,
I can hear it from down the street.
Wonder if the kids in ten of the homes around us
are able to sleep.

I imagine stealing their big screen TV. I can see it every time when I walk by simultaneously pacing and contemplating if I should ask them to *please* quiet down.

I imagine how good surround
that I can't afford, would sound
with that PHAT screen in my living room.

THAT WE SHOULDN'T BE

I wonder if it would tune out their music,
or the Ghost of Tenants Past, or the sound
of police stopping the residents they are busy blaming for the theft.

Ya know, the brown ones
who will "match the description."

It's November on Gold Street
and I just want to focus on the leaves.

    But I already know   they want us   to leave.

Until then
I will play with the children
while they are still here.

I will create a symphony of laughter
that rattles windows
awaking college students from hangover-coated slumbers.

I will make them wish we would quiet down.
I will show the neighbors that we don't have to be quiet,
that we shouldn't be.

[RACE TOGETHER]

They expect us to

        Race Together. Weather
        the storm.

But you
cannot do

        chin ups with bootstraps
        when Polos and Timbs
        are the norm.

They expect us
to change

        what's wrong; times
        have changed, so change
        the song.

    "Get up, stand up,
      stand up for your rights!"

We deserve a
community,   (unity) Say it!

In Egypt, Black was Wealthy.
In Grand Rapids, Wealthy was Black.

How quick
the images
portrayed change   when the directors are
                             "colorblind" to the "What happ's"
                             only see the "Riff-Raff"
                             a Fitted to a Snap Back.

A Sammy's Pita
and a Fresh Taper Fade
-vs-   the grave
                                  of more minority-owned business

But at least the tombstone is clean,
right? Let's chisel
"Organic Market" in it.
Label it a community staple.
Call it "*much* needed community development"!

Smile
to the neighbors

as we cut the ribbon. Let's at least
                    wave them farewell
                    shall we? Bid them a-due when their rent is.

Maybe I'm being
petty. Childish.
Let's be childish, as our youth
doesn't get to be.

Black businesses
will be the Trading Cards
nobody wants: Little Caesar's for a Sandman's?
                     Black Jack no Trade Back.
                     Finders keepers losers weepers...

But *please*,
not so loud
that you disturb the community...

A week ago I saw someone say that
Minority Business Incentives were racist.
Excuse me: "Reverse Racism".

Nothing, it's Useless

Racism Reversed as in us doing what you created?
I call it evening the odds.
Odd enough, it isn't even;
even when it appears to be.

I said: odd enough it isn't even,
even when it appears to be.

    "Get UP, stand UP,
       stand UP for YOUR Rights".

They expect us to

                    Race Together. Weather
        the storm.

I asked a sixteen-year-old Black boy last year: "What can we do to fix racism in our community, how can you fix the way people perceive you?"

His response: "Nothing, it's useless."

Last week, I smoked a cigarette
outside of Mulligan's Pub.

I laughed at how
expensive a pack   as I peered down the street
                                at the new apartments
                                I can't afford, next to the street
                                I used to live on, a corner away
                                from where I used to get my hair cut.

That boy's response in class
is the same response I'm guessing
his parents would give me.

[Handwritten in orange marker across the page: "No Du rags", "No sagging Pants", "No bandanas"]

Give me
something to show them...to prove
them wrong. Please.

                         I would keep
                                showing them myself, but I know
                                that I am a part of a system that
                                wants me to fail...

Yesterday I went to Farrah's Bar.
The owner
greeted me with a
smile. The door
patted me on the back
with a sign that said

                                Hats on straight
                                No Du-rags
                                No sagging pants
                                No bandanas

That boy who said "Nothing"
isn't welcome there.
The sign says so.

Two years ago,
I was told by a bouncer at The B.O.B
that I "didn't meet the dress code"...

                                I was outside smoking
                                during an event that I threw
                                that tripled their bar sales...

Maybe
I should stop going outside
to smoke, right?

I keep being given
reasons to quit, being

around areas that don't want us   as patrons.
                                                   or a part
                                                   of *their*
                                                   community

But that's why
I have to stay.
That
is why I *have*
to be here;

                                                   why *we* have to
                                                   be here,
                                                   so *we*
                                                   can *be*
                                                   the change.

But also, this is exausting and forced labor that feels designed to break us.

[TOUR LOG]

Chasing dreams is like chasing dragons, right?

11/24/17

> Danny,
> I love you.
> Thank you for being an inspiration.

Tomorrow I along with my tour mate am gearing up to close out the final leg of my second national tour, 'The Unpacking Tour". Although I am excited, I can't help but feel like I am chasing dreams across the country the same way kids pursue fantastical creatures, like the ones hidden in the bedtime stories some of us never received, and the books containing way more imagination than we ever have left over as adults.

But it isn't the fact that I will be able to reach new ears and touch new hearts that has me excited to surely lose money traveling across the country. Scouring poetry venues, clubs, bars, and college campuses trying to attain "The Dream" that so many think I am living is also not what fuels my ambition.

Ya' see, this time I am running away from home and nobody knows it.

I am terrified of the person I am dating being "the one," I honestly do not know where my career is going, I have no clue how to build the work I am doing in my community to new heights, I am running from my past with a different mask on each year, and I am so terrified to continue to grow... as I have no idea where I will end up.

Also, I just received word that one of my good friends Danny Rosea, co-host of "Put Up or Shut UP" (our weekly show in Kalamazoo, MI) has gone missing. This isn't some normal occurrence, especially as he just had a newborn daughter not even months ago. I secretly hope that he went missing the same way I went "missing" in February 2015; found breath full of last night's mistakes, in a bed I didn't recognize, with a phone riddled with text messages that both pieced together my night, and simultaneously filled me with fear as I realized that people were looking for me, worrying whether I was still breathing.

I had nearly 100 notifications on Facebook that spread like wildfire from my ex-girlfriend who stated "I hadn't been home" and she was worried I "didn't make it". The truth was, I just didn't make it home to her.

And honestly, I don't wish this on his family. I just hope that it is something like this and not what everyone thinks that it could be.

I am not the best at taking the time to really feel, so... I leave.
I guess I get that from my father.

11/25/17

Today, we took off across the country, driving from Michigan to Texas on the first leg of the trip—in a 2006 Chevy Aveo, which not ironically was the first car I ever tried to purchase.

We started driving straight to Texas but a quarter of the way through the trip, somewhere in Ohio, the check oil light came on. We decided to go to a Valvoline and get a Full Service (yeah... right) Oil Change. And after we let the attendant know what was going on he responded with a not-too-reassuring, "Don't worry, we will take care of it".

So, we ended up paying $60 for an overpriced oil change—only to jump back on the highway, continue south, and at our next stop for gas—as we were pulling out of the parking a lot—the steering... wheel... barely... moved...

Turns out the power steering pump blew! We decided to voyage the rest of the way to Texas with no power steering whatsoever, this compact car steering like a cruise ship the entire rest of the way.

11/28/17

When we arrived, we decided to find another Valvoline, thinking, "Hey, these people just did a 'Full Service Check Up,' maybe they will take care of it and make it right?"

Not so much luck. Instead, this wispy-haired troll in overalls tells me "I can't fix it, but don't worry... I know a guy!" (Of course he does...) And he tells us, "It will only be $1000."

We tell him: "Absolutely not."

Mind you, this is more than we have in our checking and savings accounts combined.

So we search all over Austin, TX for mechanics that will fix it if we buy the parts ourselves, also calling all over the city for a power steering pump. And in doing so, we found this guy.

This guy reminded me of the dragonslayers you see in movies, except instead of massive bone memorials of enormous fire-breathing, flying reptiles being a beacon of pride circling his kingdom, this guy had one literally *full* of cars. It looked like a car museum and a car graveyard had a baby right in his front lawn!

This dude fixed the car for next to nothing, charged us a mere, like, $250 dollars, then actually came to our show in Austin, Texas! He bought books, shirts, CDs, and showed *us so much love*. Honestly, it was exactly what we needed to get our spirits in the right direction after the series of trash events that had us almost heading back to the place I was so eager to run away from.

John was our hero; our knight in shining armor, his dragon's skull a used power steering pump, now safely mounted in our chariot.

11/29/17

You gotta be kidding me...

Tonight, we headed to Houston. We parked the car, brought all of our stuff to the venue, and set up all of our merchandise. About twenty minutes later, Safi—the organizer of Write About Now—asked us where we parked.

We told him—"behind the venue"—to which he responded, "WE GOTTA GO GET IT, NOW!"

I was thinking, "Bro we just got it out of the shop," but he is freaking out, like, "Y'all don't understand; they tow out here like crazy!"

So frantically we run to the car, and: just our luck, there is no car there. In not even thirty minutes, they towed it.

After sulking back to the venue we rocked the show. It was incredible, and the crowd showed us *so much love*. We actually made just enough to pay the stupid $750 it took to get the car *out* of the impound lot.

Normally, you go into grassroots tours with the intention of not always making all of your money back, but this... this is ridiculous.

Today might have been the final straw in this metaphorical camel's back.

Not to mention, they found Danny. His body was in the Kalamazoo River.

I can feel myself crashing, my soul is on fire, all I want to do is cry.

12/1/17

We left Texas, all "we gotta get the hell out of here" like, and decided to drive through the night to our shows in Colorado.

Let me just say, there are a few hundred miles between Amarillo, Tx and Colorado—somewhere in New Mexico—that might be the most beautiful place on earth; a secret location where my sanity still resides that is a strange mixture of ghost towns, rock faces, mountains, and ranch country.

Here is where I came to terms with the fact that Dany Rosea is no longer with us, that by touring, I was missing his funeral and wouldn't be there to console our community. Here, where it was so quiet that the only thing that sung louder than the overt racism oozing out of the pores of gas station attendants was the feeling of helplessness when nothing around you screams *home*, or feels familiar.

The air is much, much clearer there, so clear that I finally feel that I can breathe. If only one deep breathe.

When we got to Colorado Springs an hour before our show, we had to park the car so we could ask for directions. And wouldn't you know it: steam starts bellowing out of the hood as soon as we stop, almost as if the car was trying to make smoke signals or cloud formations or something like that. It was stupid.

At this point, we are defeated; and then my tournamte realizes they "think they left their wallet at the tiny Mexican restaurant" somewhere after the place that looked like God's Country.

My road trip partner is crying. I am trying to remain calm. I propose that we "just rock this show, get a hotel, and in the morning, we will call a mechanic." Little did we know that in Colorado Springs, they are the real "God's Country" and the entire town practically shuts down on Sunday...

The show was great, and we ended up staying at the world's sketchiest hotel—a Knights Inn—that had to have had bed bugs (or scabies at least). We woke up the next morning to a *beautiful* view of the mountains. When we arrived, the blackness must have been oozing out of our minds and into the sky, as it was so dark that we would have never known we were surrounded by such a truly breathtaking view.

We called a mobile mechanic to meet us at our car—apparently the only one who worked on Sundays. We jumped in an Uber to go back to the car, and when we arrived...

The doors were open, the trunk was open, and someone had stolen everything we owned.

Everything. From coats & clothes, to yoga mats, to snacks, and even merchandise.

It was all gone. Gone. The mechanic who met us there asked, "is this how you left it?"

I honestly just wanted to break down, but instead we told him the story of everything that had happened in the last few days. He shook his head and just went to work fixing it. At the end, he told us he wouldn't accept our money.

He got our car in better working order then it was before we started, and said, "Ya know what, you both just keep sharing your story, because I know someone needs to hear it."

"Keep paying it forward, inspiring people to do the same" he said.

That is when I realized that we were never hunting down success, fame, or the capturing of hearts on this tour, but growth. We were chasing dreams, the same way people say that knights would pursue the most vicious of dragons. The struggles, hardships, and grief became another claw on our neck or tooth on our sword; a token that even the scariest of things can become part of our destiny, and that, through the fire, we evolve.

This trip has changed our lives. He saved us. And we made it back to Michigan, but not without leaving memories of Danny at every step of the way.

This story was originally told for the New Holland Brewing Company Dragon's Milk #ShareALegend Campaign.

[BUTTERFLY]

So now I'm sitting there
watching this Animal Planet show about butterflies.

                                            Because who can stay upset
when looking at butterflies, right?

Yet there I was: a Snot Tear Extravaganza
Ugly Face Cherry-On-Top
sprinkled with that hideous
Dying Lion Seal Noise
(the one people make when they are really upset)
crying my eyes out.

                                                       I can laugh about it now,
because I learned about the cycle.

It starts with feeding:
destroying and engulfing
the very things that gave it life.

                                                      The same way I did my mother.

The same way I proceed to with lovers,
friends, my environment, and people
that unknowingly become new leaves
for me to turn over when I crave destruction
not yet willing to taking it out on myself.

                                                   Though I always do
somehow they are always kind enough
to take me back
everytime I metabolize them, and shed
dead layers of myself.

>   Though I don't deserve it
>   they often follow it with a
>   *You should be so proud of how much you've grown.*
>   but I never am.

They don't know that each time,
my hunger evolves alongside me. It becomes larger.

I strive to take up more space
no matter how minute I feel.

Every time I feel even close to "big enough"
I stop eating, fill myself on excuses.
I forgot
Today I was too busy
and, worst: *I don't deserve it*

Until I pick a spot under a covered location. The documentary called this "The Pupa Stage".

>   Is my couch not a chrysalis or cocoon?
>   The bathroom floor,
>   the bed in the guest room
>   away from the woman I love...
>
>   the places I lock myself away for days
>   from nurture. Are they not
>   that protective layer, the place
>   I wrap myself in to feel whole
>   before breaking into nothing
>   so I feel safe enough to spread my wings?

When you are laying there motionless
this is when your mind does
nature's magic, body still
metabolizing itself.

After days, I emerge:
that Vibrant Flowing Being
that so many see.

                                       When battling anxiety,
                                                   bi-polar,
                                               and depression,
                                                  ask yourself:

isn't it strange
how a caterpillar's transformation
into a butterfly
can look so much
like me?

ACKNOWLEDGMENTS AND NOTES

For Nika Marie Price, my forever love.

For Jacobi & Taylor, but especially Gracen.

For every young person that saw themselves in me.

For every teacher that trusted me with their students.

For every person who has done wrong, and works to be better.

For those, like me, that society deems to be uneducated, unqualified, and nothing more than their criminal history or the skeletons they are most ashamed of.

For the do-ers, and the dreamers, for the ceiling breakers, and those still struggling to piece themselves together. The ones who strive to show those that call ideas impossible Possible.

For those who inspired me to live, when I was ready to stop; Martel, Foster, Brandon, Mitch, Tamara,

Tamara, Tamara, and especially Tamara. For Baxter, Mila, Adrian, Bryce, LT, LaDawn, and Momma Melvene.

For my Grandmother, one of very few to ever truly love me unconditionally; and to all of those that stopped me on the street, in the coffee shop, at the grocery store and told me to keep my head up, when I was drowning in darkness...

Thank you, because YOU saved ME, from me.

Crossworm (Steve Weatherbie), who designed the guts of this book and also mastered the audio version. You are my favorite Canadian, ever. Thank you for pushing me, that uber ride changed my life.

Ander Monson, who took a leap of faith with this project, me, and who laboriously brought this to life. Michigan loses too many truly remarkable people and the university that did not retain you f**ked up.

It has been a joy to talk alongside you; which also goes to say, P. Smith—I adore you, this wouldn't be possible without you!

Jay Jackson, who scored all of the audio, and also mixed this project—you text back terribly, but you might be one of the most prolific Michigan artists I have ever met. And I feel lucky to have met you.

Piper Adonya, who designed the images that separate each chapter. You are exceptional! The world doesn't even know yet, but they will.

Esan Sommersell, who masterfully did the cover art. Thank you, for being you. Honest. Raw. Flawed.

Beautiful. Remarkable Black man, regardless of if you are given the tools, and the resources—you will shine. No one besides you will ever stop your radiance.

Ryan Rayne, who recorded this entire project. This, has been a long time coming. But because of all of this Michigan Talent... *New American Monarch* has arrived. Thank you for giving this project wings.

NEW MICHIGAN PRESS, based in Tucson, Arizona, prints poetry and prose chapbooks, especially work that transcends traditional genre. Together with DIAGRAM, NMP sponsors a yearly chapbook competition.

DIAGRAM, a journal of text, art, and schematic, is published bimonthly at THEDIAGRAM.COM. Periodic print anthologies are available from the New Michigan Press at NEWMICHIGANPRESS.COM.

MARCEL FABLE PRICE is a multi-hyphenate, self-directed, intuitive creative whose primary medium is stranded somewhere between oratory expression and creative writing.

Fable is the 2016 recipient of a Community Advocate Award, 2017 40 Under 40 Honoree, was the 2017-2020 Poet Laureate of Grand Rapids, MI, a 2020 Grand Rapids area Black Businesses "Black Bottom Community Builder" Award winner, 2021 Michigan Humanities Impact Partner of the Year, 2022 Newsmaker of the Year, and was given the "Imagination Award" by the West Michigan Center for Arts and Technology in 2023.

Fable was the youngest, the first person without a college degree, and the first person of color to hold the title of Poet Laureate in Grand Rapids, MI.

His work is a kaleidoscope of personal experiences, crafted into stained glass examples of transformation desired to connect with readers in a painstakingly beautiful way regardless of their own lived experience. Fable truly believes the mortar to our humanity is shared experience and without intentionally searching for ways to connect, our individual gospels will only remain surface hymns.

His work has previously been used by PBS, The Frey Foundation, Mental Health America, and Habitat for Humanity. He has graced the cover of *Grand Rapids Magazine*, and his poems have appeared in *The Missouri Review*, *Button Poetry*, and *Write About Now*.

❉

COLOPHON

Text is set in a digital version of Jenson, designed by Robert Slimbach in 1996, and based on the work of punchcutter, printer, and publisher Nicolas Jenson. The titles here are also in Jenson.

www.ingramcontent.com/pod-product-compliance
Lightning Source LLC
Chambersburg PA
CBHW062114080426
42734CB00012B/2857